The Man with the
Beautiful Voice

Also by Lillian B. Rubin, Ph.D.

Dr Lillian B. Rubin

THE MAN WITH THE BEAUTIFUL VOICE

*And More Stories from
the Other Side of the Couch*

PIATKUS

Visit the Piatkus website!

Piatkus publishes a wide range of bestselling fiction and non-fiction, including books on health, mind body & spirit, sex, self-help, cookery, biography and the paranormal.

If you want to:

- read descriptions of our popular titles
- buy our books over the internet
- take advantage of our special offers
- enter our monthly competition
- learn more about your favourite Piatkus authors

VISIT OUR WEBSITE AT: www.piatkus.co.uk

Copyright © 2003 by Lillian B. Rubin

First published in the USA in 2003 by Beacon Press.

First published in Great Britain in 2004 by
Piatkus Books Limited
5 Windmill Street
London W1T 2JA
e-mail: info@piatkus.co.uk

The moral right of the author has been asserted

*A catalogue record for this book is
available from the British Library*

ISBN 0 7499 2414 8

Printed and bound in Great Britain by
CPI Bath, Bath, Somerset

For My Patients
Who taught me much of what I know

Contents

The Man with the
Beautiful Voice

Doing Therapy

It's my first day at the clinic where I'm about to begin my internship, the necessary prelude to getting licensed as a psychotherapist. A momentous day for me, routine for everyone else, so there's no fuss or ceremony to welcome me on board. Instead, after a brief meeting with my supervisor, who tells me how he expects me to be prepared for our biweekly sessions, a secretary shows me to the office I'll use, tells me how to get an outside line on the phone, points out the panic button on the wall just to the right of my chair, and leaves me with the chart for my first patient, a twenty-eight-year-old man named Mike who, according to the intake report, suffers from acute anxiety.

I'm excited as I lead him down the hall from the waiting room to my office, eager to begin this work I've chosen. He's tall, probably a little over six feet, good-looking in a rugged sort of way, his square face, lined beyond his years, framed by unruly dark hair, his eyes an unreadable smoky black. He hesitates when we walk into the office, looks around as if wondering what he's doing here, and for a moment I think he's going to turn and leave. But he takes my cue when I point to a chair and drops into it, slouching down so deeply that his neck is invisible and his head seems to sprout directly out of his shoulders. Despite the warm spring day he's wearing a bulky down jacket, which he keeps zipped up to his chin, and his hands are jammed into his pockets as if glued there.

I've read plenty of books, taken lots of classes, but none of them really prepared me for this moment, the first time I would sit in a room with another human being and think, Oh my God, this is it; somebody's life is in my hands.

I learned in my training that I must wait for the patient to begin the session, that how these opening moments are navigated, what a person chooses to start with, tell a therapist a lot. But no one ever told me what to do when a patient sits across from me immobile, except for a slight eye tic, and stares with an intensity that feels as if his eyes are boring holes in my head. I shift around in my chair, uncomfortable, off stride, my fragile confidence ebbing as the silence in the room becomes too heavy to bear. I know it has meaning; I know I should wait, but there's something vaguely menacing about the silence, and the minutes begin to feel very long. So I finally ask what brought him into the clinic. He shrugs but doesn't speak. I try another tack and ask him to tell me something about himself.

His eyes flicker away and, talking down into his jacket so that I have to strain forward to hear him, he volunteers only that he's a student at the university and also works part-time but has just been fired from his job.

"Do you want to talk about that?" I ask.

He's agitated, but not enough to raise any alarms, as he tells me that his boss is "an asshole," that "he was always looking to get me on something," and that "he finally found some fucking excuse to fire me. The motherfucking asshole was out to get me from the beginning," he concludes.

I'm not sure what, if any, response to make, so I ask, "How are you doing in school?"

He looks at me warily, "Why are you asking me about that?"

Taken aback, I think for a moment. I've been taught that I should turn his question back to him by asking what about my query is a problem for him. But something tells me not to do it, that my only chance with this guy is to answer him honestly, so I say, "Because the two things you told me are that you're a student and that you were fired from your job. Clearly the job part of your life hasn't been going so well, so I'm wondering about the school part."

He looks somewhat relieved and, although still tense and uncomfortable, begins to talk a bit about his life at school. He's apparently an apt student, not top of the class but good enough. Some days, he says, he feels okay about school; other days he doesn't.

So far, so good, I tell myself, pleased that he seems to be opening up. "Any idea what happens on the days you don't?"

His agitation returns, "How the hell should I know; it's because of them."

"Who?"

He retreats to silence, only this time he isn't staring at me. Instead he looks like a trapped animal, his eyes darting around the room, his body suddenly upright and tense as if on guard against an attack. I wait a few heartbeats then say, "You look upset. Do you want to talk about it?"

"What for?" he growls. "You won't believe me either. Nobody believes that they're after me, but I know they're there, just waiting."

"Try me," I say encouragingly.

But by then he's gone, unable to hear anything but what's going on in his own head. He continues to rant, his words soon becoming an incoherent stream, while I sit transfixed, my thoughts leaping around uselessly. This guy is really crazy. So what did you think, that you'd be seeing only sane people? Never mind that, what do I do now? Before I have a chance to figure out my next move, he pulls a short-bladed knife from his pocket and slams it repeatedly into the arm of his chair while screaming about "those motherfucking bastards" and promising "to get them."

I'm afraid to speak, afraid to move, afraid to sit still. After what seems like forever but is probably only seconds, I remember the panic button, reach down, and push it. Almost immediately two men storm into in my office and are all over Mike.

I hear later that they took him to the inpatient ward, where he was diagnosed with *paranoid schizophrenia* (a diagnosis that doesn't bode well for a return to sustained normal functioning) and held for treatment. Which means essentially that he'll be medicated and kept there until he shows no more obvious symptoms, then released. The rest is predictable. Once out from under hospital supervision, he'll most likely stop taking the medication that stabilized him, complaining that it makes him feel like a zombie (which is probably true when compared to his highly energized paranoid state), and pretty soon he'll be back again in a continuing cycle of hospitalization and release.

When the chaos in the clinic subsides, I'm summoned to meet with my supervisor, a seasoned psychoanalyst. He listens closely to my detailed recounting of the session, then chastises me for breaking the rule that says a therapist should wait to see what's on the patient's mind before speaking. "It's a technical error that can have serious consequences for the course of therapy as I hope you've just learned."

A technical error? The language chills me. A mistake in an architect's calculations of the strength of a weight-bearing beam, the wrong command to a computer that brings up the dreaded *fatal error* message, these are technical errors. But to speak of a technical error when I had just witnessed an intelligent and seemingly normal young man fall into the kind of uncontrollable paranoia that could allow him to kill struck me as beyond absurd. Where was a teacher when I needed one, someone who could help me to understand what had happened in that room, someone with enough experience — no, not just experience, wisdom — to apprehend the terror that underlay Mike's paranoia, someone with enough empathy for a budding therapist to grasp the anxious disorientation and terrible impotence I was feeling?

It's more than thirty years since that day, but I've never forgotten how helpless I felt when I left my supervisor's office. True, he was an inordinately rigid man, more extreme in his response than others who came later might have been. But he wasn't alone in teaching that psychotherapy is a science and emphasizing technique as if a course of therapy would stand or fall on the perfect interpretation, the ingenious intervention, the well-timed silence.

Such interventions do have their uses; they are some of the tools we need to do our work. But they're just that, tools that at best are useful only in the hands of a therapist skilled in the art of relatedness. I understood then, as I do now, that the therapeutic relationship is different from others, that because of its special nature and the kind of emotional intensity it generates, some rules are necessary to help bind behavior on both sides. But even then I also understood that to turn good reasons into rock-hard edicts is to set up a rigid formula for behavior that's antithetical to everything we know about how to build a relationship that, whether in psychotherapy or in life, rests on the comfort of knowing we're understood and the trust that such knowledge will never be used against us.

Although I was already a seasoned adult with plenty of experience in the world of human relationships (becoming a therapist was a midlife career change for me), it took years of struggle to push those who were my teachers, whether in the classroom or in the books they wrote, off my shoulder and out of the room, years when I searched for a way to do this work that felt authentic to me, that honored those rules that make sense (never cross the boundary between intimacy and a sexual interaction, for example) and cast aside those that don't (never touch a patient or, God forbid, accept a hug). And it was even longer before I dared speak about what I actually do once the door is closed and it's just we two, my patient and I.

I'm not alone in this experience. Any thoughtful therapist has stories about how she broke "the rules" but never dared tell. So deeply embedded in the therapeutic culture is this conflict between theory and practice that some of the most rigid upholders of the rules, training analysts at various psychoanalytic institutes who threaten their students with expulsion for any deviation, often behave quite differently in the privacy of their consulting rooms. For despite what they may teach, they know that if they're to be effective, they have no choice but to enter the therapeutic encounter with the kind of humility that opens the possibility for the emergence of a meaningful relationship between two people, both of whom struggle in their own ways (although the patient more openly so than the therapist) to meet life's uncertainties.

Not that they're on even terrain. Therapists do have some expertise to offer patients in that struggle, some knowledge, some way of seeing a problem and analyzing it that sheds light. Their training helps, of course, but so does the fact that they are participants in life, that they are familiar in a deeply personal way with many of the issues their patients confront. It's precisely that familiarity, that knowledge born of experience, that allows for the kind of empathic responsiveness necessary to a successful therapy.

Things have changed since I entered the field, although not universally and not enough. So despite some important theoretical advances, much remains the same in practice. As I write, for example, a prominent psychoanalyst, interviewed for a *New York Times* article (February 5, 2002) about films and psychotherapy, complained that film presentations distort and stereotype the process, leaving patients with inappropriate expectations. To illustrate his point he told of a patient who, after seeing a film in which the therapist hugged a suicidal patient, requested the same of him. "It really helped him a lot," she said, "so I was wondering if you could hug me."

"That was a movie," the doctor explained. "This is therapy, and we need to use words."

"Yes, I know it was a movie," the patient replied, "but the hug helped a lot."

Who's distorted? I wondered as I read. Whose expectations are inappropriate? Why, in a moment like that, are words and a hug mutually exclusive?

I'm not advocating that therapists indiscriminately hold their patients in their arms, only that we see them as we would like to be seen. Was this woman so childlike that she was really influenced only by a scene in a film? Or did what she saw resonate with her natural yearning for connection and relatedness with someone who was an important emotional figure in her internal life?

In the continuing struggle to understand the human psyche and heal its suffering, psychoanalysis no longer reigns supreme. As the cultural upheavals of the last decades took root, new theories rose up, old ones were dusted off and revisited. Partly because of the growing competition from other therapeutic models, and partly because generations of new psychoanalytically trained clinicians rebelled against the rigidity of classical psychoanalysis, it, too, has been reinterpreted in ways that more nearly meet the needs of the contemporary world and the people who live in it.

Still, from behaviorism to systems theory to modern psychoanalysis, the view of psychotherapy as a science dominates clinical psychology and psychiatry. In reality, however, psychotherapy is a cross between science and art in which science holds sway over thought, art over practice. It can lay claim to science only if science is defined most broadly — an endeavor that proceeds from a theoretical model to the generation of hypotheses that can be tested in practice. But given that the "testing" is done by therapists who work unobserved behind closed doors, women and men who are not neutral observers but thinking, feeling human beings who bring with them their own problems, their own views of the world, their own beliefs, and their own unique ways of seeing and hearing, the tests are not and never can be the controlled, systematic, and rigorous inquiries that science requires.

It's true, of course, that science at its creative best involves a level of artfulness that may leap beyond the norms, a leap that is most likely to be successful in the hands of an accomplished and experienced scientist. And it's also true that art has its rules, as every artist knows. It's possible, for example, to draw a human face by following the rules set out in any book of instruction. But turning that face into an artistic production, a portrait that not only resembles the subject but reveals something of her inner life and personality, this takes a level of creativity that can't be so easily taught.

In psychology the need to formulate unyielding rules grows out of a complicated mix of forces related to the nature of the psychotherapeutic enterprise and the kind of training that's necessary. No matter how many classroom lectures and case seminars a student attends by way of preparation, ultimately it's in doing therapy that he becomes a therapist. Training, therefore, takes place on live subjects by men and women who are generally young, inexperienced, and probably as unsure of themselves as their patients are. Not surprisingly, then, no responsible professional wants to send a neophyte into a room with a troubled human being without some guidelines that circumscribe what can happen behind the closed door. But if therapy is more art than science, no external directives can overcome the reality that it's an art that needs time and experience, both in the psychotherapeutic encounter and in life itself, to reach its full development.

I don't mean to turn psychotherapy into a mystical endeavor for which there can be no training. My point is only that the disciplinary insistence that it's a science gives rise to the kind of teachings that are responsible for some of its greatest mistakes and worst abuses, among them the promulgation of rules for behavior that inhibit rather than facilitate an effective therapeutic relationship.

It's the psychotherapy-as-science view that's responsible for the ubiquitous practice of pinning a diagnostic label on a person that in itself points the way to the "correct" therapeutic path, like a doctor prescribing an antibiotic for a strep throat. Yet in more than three decades of clinical practice, I've never seen a person who fit neatly into any diagnostic category, an observation that's given weight beyond my own experience by the continuing attempts at ever greater specificity in diagnosis. So, for example, where we once diagnosed *borderline personality*, we now have several subcategories (borderline personality with narcissistic features or with hysterical features, to name just two) that serve only to emphasize how slippery such categories are. For no matter how carefully we refine them, these labels are no more than heuristic devices that, although they may aptly describe a collection of symptoms and behaviors, cannot do justice to the person sitting in the other chair.

It's easy to blame the rise of HMOs, with their demand for clear diagnoses and treatment plans, for the rush to diagnosis among clinicians. But while there's some truth in the charge, the greater truth is that insurers only hastened and consolidated a trend that, as psychology sought to establish itself as a science, was already well under way long before HMOs held such power over the delivery of health services.

The need to promote itself as a science is rooted in both the sociology and psychology of the discipline. At the sociological level, all professions develop a language that becomes a convenient shorthand its practitioners use when talking among themselves. It's part of the process by which a profession institutionalizes itself, a way of claiming its expertise and defining its boundaries, a way of assuring that outsiders are kept out. Where, in addition, the knowledge base of a field is shaky and vulnerable to varying interpretations, it becomes imperative to offer what seems like empirical evidence that demonstrates its scientific validity to itself and to the world. In sociology, the other field in which I've been trained, we turn to statistics and mathematical models, quantifying the unquantifiable in the hope that we'll be permitted entry into the halls of hard science. In psychology we diagnose. The ability to do so is "proof" that we, too, are practitioners of a science that deserves an honored place in the medical hierarchy and, not incidentally, qualifies us for insurance coverage. And the "proof" lies in the *DSM IV* (*Diagnostic and Statistical Manual of Mental Disorders, 4th edition*), the diagnostic bible of mental health professionals that minutely details the criteria for each of hundreds of mental illnesses that run the gamut from serious psychoses to relatively benign adjustment disorders.

But it's not just some abstract professional desire to be seen as scientific that makes the labeling process so pervasive and so dangerous. This is one of those moments when the requirements of the discipline meet the psychological anxieties of its practitioners who need something to hold on to, something to point the way out of the confusion of data and emotion that fill the room. A diagnostic label serves to calm the therapist's apprehension about the messiness of the therapeutic process by giving shape to an experience that, without it, is often bewildering. Unfortunately, the label isn't just an organizing tool; it slots a person into a category that embodies within it a set of treatment imperatives, a list of do's and don'ts that frames the course of the therapy.

Never mind that the diagnosis may have only a tenuous relationship to a patient's problems or that, even if it has some validity, different therapeutic perspectives prescribe different treatment plans. Never mind that such labeling focuses the therapist on pathology and obscures those parts of the patient that exist in all of us and rise above any category we might devise. Never mind, either, that diagnostic fads come and go, so that what we call *borderline personality disorder* today, with all that word implies for treatment, may be viewed through an entirely different lens five years from now.

It's true that, regardless of how they're labeled, this and other disorders do exist, and they need treatment. But it's also true that the naming itself has consequences, both positive and negative, for the practice of therapy. On the positive side, naming allows us to see what was formerly hidden. On the negative, given the elusiveness and ambiguity of clinical data, once a disorder is "discovered" and labeled, it's easy to see it everywhere we look. Pretty soon it develops a life of its own, even generating a whole industry of workshops and seminars to teach therapists how to spot and treat it.

Remember the *repressed memory syndrome*? We don't hear much about it anymore, but it was big news a few years ago, and therapists too often encouraged patients to spend years looking for what wasn't there. Who hasn't heard of *ADD* (*attention deficit disorder*) or *ADHD* (*attention deficit hyperactive disorder*), which followed closely on its heels and ratcheted the seriousness up? Both are diagnoses that generally call for Ritalin, a powerful drug that has been widely prescribed for children (usually boys) whose only symptom may be that they're more active than their teachers and parents would like. Then there's the recent vogue in *multiple personality disorder* (reincarnated now as *dissociative disorder*), a rare psychological phenomenon that, if we're to judge by the rate of diagnoses, suddenly became increasingly common a few years ago.

The temptation to reach for a diagnosis, for something that promises to organize what feels like chaos, is a powerful one from which few therapists are immune, I no more than others. So there were times, especially in the early years but even sometimes later when, in the beginning stages of a particularly difficult therapy, affixing a label to the patient gave me something to grasp, something that seemed to give meaning to what was happening before me. But the impulse was born of my own need for order and control rather than the immediate needs of the therapy. In fact, those periods of uncertainty were the very times when, if I could have sat still and lived with my anxiety, I might have understood a lot sooner that the confusion was itself a clue to something important about my patient, myself, and our interaction. For whatever else therapy may be, whatever wisdom or insight a therapist may offer a patient, however much we may probe the unconscious, the heart of therapy is in the relationship. It's what happens between two thinking, feeling people in the room — how well the therapist is able to understand not just the patient's conflicts but her own, how the transference-countertransference feelings that every relationship stirs are attended to — that makes therapy work.

If it's the relationship that heals, then clearly each therapy must be tailored to it, a process that doesn't lend itself to easy categories and rigid rules. Instead, good psychotherapy is a course in unfolding, an exploration in which the therapist is a guide with an often unsteady hand. For much as we understand about the nature of the conflicts that bedevil our patients, acute as our intuitive antennae may be, good as we may be at forging relationships, every therapist knows what it's like to sit across from a patient feeling baffled and unable to make sense of what's happening in the room. It's precisely at those moments that we need to proceed with the most caution, to rein in the normal tendency to make sense of *non*-sense by affixing a label that must, by its very nature, do violence to the fullness of the person before us and threatens to leave us blinded to the other "selves," the parts that aren't yet clearly visible and that it's our job to unearth and elevate.

Some therapies are easy, the patient requiring only the lightest touch, the slightest push to go down into the deeper levels of her internal world. These are the ones for which a therapist gives thanks. Others are more difficult, leaving both therapist and patient anxious and frustrated as they fumble and stumble in search of clues that will lead them to understanding. Most are somewhere in between, sessions in which week after week the patient recites the problems of his external life without being able to probe very deeply into his internal one. For me, at least, these give the most trouble since they don't bring the rewards and excitement that come from working with the easy ones, nor do they offer the challenge of the difficult ones.

Like most therapists I work against my negative feelings, trying to sort out why I feel the way I do, striving to distinguish what's my issue from what belongs to the patient in the hope that I can use the information to facilitate the work of therapy. But in the final analysis, I know that, as with anyone else, my attachment is strongest to those people who interest me. Sometimes it's because the work itself raises some special theoretical or clinical problems, sometimes because the person is particularly stimulating emotionally or intellectually. Sometimes, it's because the patient does the work easily and makes me feel competent, sometimes because he touches something inside me in some way I can't always define. And sometimes a patient holds a special place in my heart because with her I learn something important about myself.

For therapy is not a one-way affair. We don't just "treat" patients as the patient-therapist model suggests. It's a process that forces us to confront ourselves in unexpected and often difficult ways. And in the giving-getting exchange of therapy it's safe to say that I've gotten as much as I've given, and that my patients deserve credit for a good part of my own growth and development over these past decades.

After more than thirty years and hundreds of patients, I know the limits of psychotherapy as well as of my own skills. I know my strengths and weaknesses, the places where I can see with a kind of blazing clarity and those where I'm blinded by a combination of my past experience, my present situation, and the needs, not always conscious, that spring from both. I know, too, that therapy often promises more than it can deliver, not because therapists think they're godlike, not even because the theory itself holds out the hope that if we look hard enough, long enough we can find the source of our pain and erase it (although that's a very big contributor), but also because we as a nation have mistaken our constitutional guarantee of the *pursuit* of happiness for the promise of it.

This book is about *doing* therapy rather than being in it. We have plenty of patients' accounts of their therapy but, with a few notable exceptions, the experience from the other side of the couch tends to be shrouded in mystery, protected by the myths psychology has built around itself and by the conspiracy of silence with which we try to shield ourselves and our profession from critical appraisal.

There are case studies in the professional literature, of course, often chilly, distanced presentations filled with professional jargon that obscures the human drama that's the essence of psychotherapy and that focus almost exclusively on the patient's pathology and the therapist's interventions designed to "fix" it. It's true that the more modern schools of dynamic psychology and psychoanalysis recognize that the therapeutic encounter is a social construction with two actors in the room who together create a small social system that affects their behavior. But their accounts, too, generally are presented with cool detachment and a vocabulary that speaks of *subjectivities* and *intersubjectivity*, abstract concepts that violate the very spirit of what they say they understand and that allow the therapist to hide behind a jargon that obscures rather than illuminates the feelings that are an inevitable part of his internal process.

The stories that follow, cases drawn from my clinical practice, are about what it took to become an effective therapist after I was stamped and certified with a license.* They're about trying to find my own way in my own voice, about learning what of my training was useful, what I had to discard, about when and how I could bend or break the rules safely. I've learned in these years about the balance of giving and getting for therapist and patient, about the anxieties and conflicts the therapeutic relationship can stir, about what it takes to manage those conflicts and how difficult it can be. All together they offer a view from the other side of the couch that, I hope, will give both patient and therapist a clearer understanding of the therapeutic process, its problems and its possibilities.

---

*All the stories are true, and in the interest of preserving patient confidentiality, all the names and other identifying information have been changed.

The White Hat

I can still see her as she was when I opened the door to my waiting room on her first visit, a small woman, shoulders hunched as if protecting against the cold, her body wrapped in a long dark coat two sizes too big and far too warm for the balmy fall day, and on her head, a small-brimmed white cotton hat jammed so low that it all but obscured her face. With her head bent low she mumbled an unintelligible response to my greeting and scurried past me, reminding me of a mouse as it scoots across the floor. By the time I'd closed the door and made my way across the room, she had plopped into a chair, where she sat slumped over, her eyes downcast, her fingers drumming steadily on her knees. Strange, I thought; she sounded perfectly normal when we spoke on the phone a week ago.

At moments like this I wonder sometimes how I got myself into this business. I'm reminded of a friend whose immigrant mother came to visit him when he was doing his psychiatric residency. As she toured the wards with him, she became more and more agitated until finally she burst out, "Tony, you can't work here. You went to school to be a doctor, these are crazy people!"

I know why I'm here, just as he knew. In one way or another every therapist probably is drawn to the work as much to deal with his own internal issues as with those of the people who sit in the other chair. And indeed, I have at least as much reason to thank my patients for teaching me about myself as they may have to feel grateful to me.

Now, as I looked at the woman sitting before me, I tried to remember that I'm usually glad to be here. "It's for the sun," she said, straightening up and pulling off her hat. "My face can't be in the sun," she explained as she fell back into the chair, her chin once again on her chest.

"Eva," I began, "can you . . ."

She interrupted. "Eve," she barked angrily, "it's Eve, not Eva." Then with an almost childlike mischievous smile, "You might as well get it straight right now so we can be friends."

Relieved at this small sign of life and something approaching humor, I apologized and assured her I wouldn't make that mistake again. "No," she replied, peering up at me from under a furrowed brow and sounding like a cranky child, "but you'll make lots of others."

I laughed. "Yes, that's probably true, and you'll undoubtedly call me on every one."

She looked up with the same puckish smile I'd seen earlier, visibly relaxed, and began to speak normally. We covered the usual ground for a first hour: her background, her parents, her siblings, her difficult and lonely childhood and adolescence. Now, at thirty-nine, Eve Gordon lived a life of virtual isolation. She was smart, capable, successful on the job, but a disaster in the social sphere. She ran a business out of her home doing payroll for small businesses and professional people, work that, once she got the client, required almost no further face-to-face contact. The few people she knew, women who had made overtures to her at one time or another, had dropped away because she was "never good at friendship."

As we came close to the end of the session, she began to sink into her sulky child mode and wanted to know if she'd "have to go soon." I said she would, but that we could meet again next week. At that she flopped around in the chair and shouted in a child's voice, "I thought we were going to be friends."

Inside a voice said wearily, Uh-oh, what are you getting yourself into? Do you really want to take this on? I was already struggling with some patients where the work was hard and often unrewarding; I was in the middle of writing a difficult book; and I yearned for some time to myself. But there was something compelling in her plaintive plea for a friend, perhaps because I could still remember so well my own childhood and adolescence when I, too, wasn't "good at friendship."

A therapist isn't a friend, of course, any more than a parent of a small child is, or ought to be. But this wasn't the time to take that on. Instead, I responded to the child's voice in Eve's angry plea. "Yes, Eve, I hope we can be friends, too, but friends have to say good-bye when it's time."

"Okay," she said, her eyes downcast, her chin back on her chest, "but I can't wait a whole week."

I struggled with myself for a few seconds. Did I want to see her sooner? I didn't, nor did I have another free hour that week. But I've never figured out how to send someone away once I've seen them, since I know that no matter what reason I give, it will be experienced as a rejection. And despite my misgivings, I couldn't do that to this woman who seemed like such a needy child. So I suggested another session three days later.

"That's still too long," she said petulantly, and burrowed deeper into the chair.

"I know," I said as I rose from my chair and crossed the few feet to hers, "but it's the best I can do, and you really do have to go now."

Still she didn't move until finally I reached down, took her arm, and urged her to her feet. She pulled away from my touch angrily and rushed out of the room, leaving me feeling caught between relief and concern — relief because she was gone, concern because she was a deeply troubled woman who needed help. Was there something I could have said, anything I might have done, that would have allowed her to leave more comfortably? Would she come back? Did I want her to?

Three days later my questions were answered when the bell

rang announcing her arrival. But if I had any illusion that our first session would have some effect on how she would present herself next time, it was quickly shattered when I opened the door. She darted past me without so much as a nod, but instead of sitting in the chair, she wedged herself into the corner behind it and sat hugging her knees to her chest and glowering at me defiantly as if to say "You can't make me move."

This was a first. I'd seen plenty of weird behavior, people unable to sit still, pacing restlessly, flailing about, but never this. I had no idea what to do about it, so I sat down in my chair and said quietly, "Eve, will you come sit in your chair, please?"

No answer. Instead she bent her head to her knees and brought her hands up to cover her ears. I wondered if I'd misjudged her, whether in my zeal not to label people, to focus more clearly on strength instead of pathology, I'd missed some elements of psychosis. But almost as quickly as the thought came, I realized it was my anxiety that asked the question and whatever I called it wouldn't change my response. And one thing was clear: this was a test to see if I could respond to some need I didn't know and couldn't really comprehend.

I waited about five minutes, then tried again. No answer, but a barely perceptible head movement said no. Another five minutes, then desperate to find some way to break through, "Eve, if you won't come up here, can I come sit with you down there?" A small nod of assent.

I sat next to her, my back against the wall, wondering what I was doing down there, thinking I'm too old for this, asking myself if this was therapy, worrying about how I could tell colleagues that I spent an hour sitting silently on the floor next to a regressed patient I hardly knew.

Although I fretted and fumed, that in fact is what we did for months. Twice a week Eve came in, curled up in her corner, and sat without speaking. Occasionally she'd raise her head and look at me with eyes that seemed to be pleading for something. But if I spoke, she quickly buried her head again. I couldn't tell at first if she took comfort from my presence next to her, since she made sure there was at least foot of physical space between us.

I'm not a person known for patience and much of the time I sat there brooding restlessly. I decided I needed consultation and sought out a well-respected colleague with thirty years of experience. She was empathic and agreed that this was an extraordinarily difficult patient but offered little that was useful to the work with Eve, largely because her analysis of the case and my approach to it was so conventional: I was taking on too much. Didn't I think I might be a little grandiose? I wasn't Eve's mother and had to learn the limits of what I could do. I had to set the boundaries of acceptable behavior and expect Eve to abide by them, else I was aiding and abetting her regression. A patient must be able to use what we can offer and if Eve couldn't because her regression was too profound, then she needed much more intensive work than anyone could do in an outpatient setting. There must be some countertransference issues that allowed me to put up with sitting silently on the floor for weeks.

Transference-countertransference — twin concepts, each describing a central part of the therapeutic relationship, but from different sides of the couch. Transference is when the patient projects or "transfers" onto the therapist feelings that in fact were born in earlier relationships. To take a very simple example, a therapist says to a patient, "I wonder why you said that?" The patient responds angrily, "Why are you criticizing me?" As we examine the interaction, it turns out that he's responding to the reality that his father was a constant, harping critical voice in his early life. That's transference.

The other side of transference is countertransference,

where the therapist experiences feelings toward the patient that come out of her own past experience and relationships. So, for example, it's entirely possible that, although reasonable and seeming to be benign, the question "I wonder why you said that?" is at least partly a response to the therapist's unconscious impatience or irritation and carries within it a latent critical message that the patient, exquisitely sensitized to criticism by his own past, gets.

Little attention was paid to countertransference when I was in training more than three decades ago, at least not by any of my supervisors all of whom were classically trained psychoanalysts. Nor was there much written in those years about it. The *analysis of the transference*, I was taught, was the centerpiece of psychotherapy. To the degree that the analytic community of that era acknowledged the existence of countertransference, it was thought to be an anomaly, the result of unresolved conflicts in the therapist that had to be rooted out with another course of psychoanalysis.

Today even the most classical psychoanalysts acknowledge that countertransference is an integral part of every therapeutic relationship, and that the continual examination of their own feelings is the crucible through which all therapists must pass if they're to master the craft to which they've committed themselves. But countertransference comes in all shapes and sizes. The feelings can be positive (I wish this patient were my son), or negative (this guy gives me the creeps). Either way they threaten to contaminate the therapy unless they're brought to the surface, examined, and understood.

Sometimes the countertransference issues can be so profound that the therapist is simply unable to work with the patient. Imagine the mother of a child killed in the Oklahoma City bombing treating Timothy McVeigh. More often the countertransference is less dramatic, therefore easier to manage, if sometimes harder to recognize. A therapist like myself, for example, who tends to be impatient and easily bored notices the feeling and asks: Is this me? Is there something in the dynamic between us? Or is this person really so distant from her emotional life that the work can only proceed at such a torturously slow pace? Most of the time it's some combination of all of the above.

These thoughts were far from my mind when I left my consultant's office feeling agitated and irritated at what seemed to me her facile use of words like *grandiosity* and *countertransference*. It isn't that I think I'm incapable of being grandiose or that I'm immune to countertransference reactions. But she never really attended to the facts of the case, to who Eve was, or took seriously my request to address the pros and cons of my unconventional interventions. Nevertheless, I weighed her advice, even tried to give Eve a slight push in the direction she suggested. But it served only to frighten Eve so badly that she missed our next session.

Part of me was relieved when she didn't show up. Good, I thought, maybe I've done all I can; maybe the conventional wisdom is in fact wisdom. But I didn't really believe it. Call it arrogance, call it hubris, call it egotism, call it determination — whatever the reasons, good and bad, I'm not good at giving up. So I phoned Eve and left a message saying I hoped to see her at our next scheduled session. She arrived and went to her customary place on the floor, where I joined her. I had no idea whether something useful was going on, but so long as she was there we had a chance.

Then one day Eve began to inch closer until, little by little, she would sometimes lean up against me and put her head on my shoulder, still without words. I ached to touch her, to put my arm around her, to offer her the comfort of my body, but I had to fight it out with those who sat on my shoulder, the people who had trained and supervised me, the consultant I had seen who I knew wouldn't approve, my colleagues, all the injunctions that say we must never touch a patient, a prohibition that's sometimes carried to appalling extremes.

A woman I saw in therapy some years ago told me such a story. She had been working with a therapist for three years when she was transferred to another city. As they were saying good-bye at the end of their last hour, my patient, in a gesture of gratitude, reached out to hug her therapist who pulled away and explained stiffly that it was inappropriate. Years later my patient wept when she told the story, feeling again the pain of rejection, the shame of humiliation.

Yet even when we don't fully believe in the norms and rules into which we're socialized in the process of becoming professionals, they aren't easy to ignore in any discipline. Less so perhaps in doing therapy because the certainty of theory so often conflicts with the ambiguity of practice. So somewhere inside me the questions can still linger: What if they're right and I'm wrong? What if I do harm? What if . . . ?

One doesn't have to be an expert in human relationships to know that there are times when words are useless and touch the only thing that will comfort. To deprive a therapist of this tool because it breaches some arbitrary boundary or because we fear the sexual implications violates everything we know about what heals. It's true that sexual attractions arise and that it's not always easy to deal with them in the often overheated intimacy of the transference-countertransference feelings therapy engenders. But it's no different from a sexual attraction in any other arena of life. We're not animals in heat; we have a choice about whether to act.

A therapist who can't keep his pants up or her skirt down shouldn't be allowed to practice. Unfortunately, no behavioral code ever stopped those who would take sexual advantage of a patient from doing so. Yet our fear of our sexual impulses and our puritanical conviction that sexual control lies only in the most rigid restraints push us to promulgate rules that hamstring our work while doing little or nothing to stop miscreants from theirs.

A couple of sessions later I won my internal battle with "them" and put my hand on Eve's shoulder. She flinched; I pulled back. "Has anyone ever hurt you?" I asked.

She shook her head vigorously.

"Are you sure?"

She nodded.

"Would you tell me if someone had?"

"No, and don't ask me that again."

Ten weeks and these were the first spoken words. But they were words and, in the end, honest ones. I was elated. I knew better than to stake too much on what felt like a magical moment, but in my excitement I forgot what I knew. So I not only congratulated myself, I felt smugly satisfied at having defied convention and won. But patients have a way of puncturing our vanity and reminding us that "pride goeth before a fall." I don't mean nothing changed; it did. Eve no longer resisted my touch. Instead when I didn't reach out quickly enough to satisfy her, she took my arm and put it around her. But she retreated to silence and I to a frustrated humility.

After a few more weeks, I'd had it. "I'm sorry, Eve, but you have to talk to me, otherwise we can't go on."

She looked up at me, her eyes widening in surprise. "You'd send me away?"

"I don't want to, but I don't know what else to do, and I'm afraid I can't sit here quietly like this for many more weeks."

"Why? I like it."

"I know you do, and I'm glad. But I get restless and impatient. It's time to take the next step. You have to sit up in the chair and talk to me."

"If I do it, can I come sit in the big chair with you?"

"We'll see, but first you have to sit in your own chair."

"Okay, I'll think about it."

At our next session instead of hurrying into the room with her head bent, she walked in, albeit tentatively and, watching me every moment, went directly to the chair where she sat perched on the edge as if ready for flight. She was nervous, but contained, not exactly adult, but the infant I'd been dealing with for so long was held in check. As I watched her, I couldn't help wondering: Had I coddled her unnecessarily? Was there some way I had unconsciously encouraged her acting out so I could be the loving, understanding mother I myself had dreamed of? Or was it that vague, unknowable, indescribable thing we call intuition, that sight that sees without seeing, that allows us to act outside of thought, that knowledge that precedes knowing and that, in the final analysis, is the hallmark of a good therapist. I preferred to believe the latter, of course, to believe that I'd given Eve what she needed to feel safe and trusting enough to take what for her was a very big step.

Eve never got comfortable in that session and, after sitting on the edge of the chair and talking haltingly for about half an hour, she retreated to her corner on the floor. I joined her, held her, told her I was pleased with how well she'd done. She reveled in the praise like a two-year-old who'd found the toilet instead of the diaper for the first time, reached up to stroke my face, and nearly purred contentedly.

As the months went by, she became increasingly relaxed in the chair, conversation flowed more freely, and the time spent in the corner diminished. She began, fitfully at first, as if she were frightened of the words themselves, to talk about her life in her family—about her mother's drunkenness, about being eight years old and coming home from school to find her passed out on the kitchen floor, about her father's alcoholic rages when he smashed the house up and put his fist through the wall, about the endless wait for dinner while her parents indulged in an evening-long "cocktail hour," about the many nights she went to bed hungry because they were too drunk to remember to feed their children.

When I asked again if her father ever hurt her, she reverted to baby talk, which she did every time a question or comment touched a psychological hot spot. "You promised you wouldn't ask me that again."

"No, I didn't; you told me not to ask you again, but I never agreed."

She glared at me and went to her corner. Only this time she didn't want me to join her. "Go away; I don't want to talk to you anymore. You're not my friend."

I was discouraged to see her slip back so quickly. It was hard not to feel angry at her, much like a mother who has done everything she can think to soothe a child who continues to cry. I tried to comfort myself with the reminder that at least she didn't leave the room altogether as she had on a couple of other occasions when she was frightened by something we were talking about. But it was a dispiriting time, coming as it did when we'd already been working together for well over a year.

She stayed in her corner for several weeks. This time I didn't join her and insisted that she talk to me, which she did reluctantly. Then one day she walked to the chair, sat down, and with a small smile said, "I can do it."

"What?"

"I can be your friend again."

"We'll need to talk about hard things," I warned.

"I know." Then, her words rushing together as if the sentence were all one long breathless word, "Myfathernohedidn'thitmebuthecameintomyroomand. . . . Idon'twanttotalkaboutit."

But at least it was said, and she stayed in the chair talking in a normal voice until, halfway through the session, she reverted to baby talk. "Lillian, if I don't go in the corner, can I come sit in the big chair with you?"

"Yes, but only after we've talked some more."

"How much more?"

"Let's wait and see; I'll tell you when."

I was struck by the juxtaposition of the two thoughts, the admission of her father's abuse and her raising the question about the corner. "Eve, did you hide in the corner at home?"

She nodded.

"To get away from your dad?"

"Can I come sit in the big chair now?"

"Soon, but I'd like you to answer my question first?"

"My mom, too, when she got mad. At night I hid in the corner of the closet so my father couldn't find me, but in the day, I just crawled behind the couch because Mom couldn't get me there."

"Did your mother hit you?"

"You promised I could sit in the big chair."

"In just another minute, Eve. But first tell me if your mother hurt you."

A slight nod of the head, then with her eyes glued to the floor, the words tumbled into each other again. "Butshedidn'tmeantosheonlydiditwhenshewasdrunk."

These are the moments every therapist waits for, the times when the frustrations and anxieties are forgotten, and we know why we do this work. We were both quiet, each preoccupied with her own reaction to the words that finally were spoken aloud, words that Eve had spent her life denying, fearing. I savored the moment and wondered what she was thinking and feeling. As if she heard my unspoken question, she lifted her head and, in a voice filled with wonder, said, "I can't believe it. I said it and nothing terrible happened. I'm still here, and God didn't strike me dumb." Then, in one of those quick switches I would probably never be quite ready for, she retreated to the child's voice. "Now can I come sit in the big chair with you, Lillian?"

"Yes," I said, moving aside to make room for her.

She curled up there while I wondered what new problems this would stir up and how I'd get her to leave. But when I told her the time was up, she just sighed, shook her head sadly, and left. Until then she had always come and gone without a word, no greeting on arrival, no good-bye on departure. This time she stopped at the door, turned back to look directly at me, and said, "Good-bye, Lillian. Thanks."

But like life, therapy doesn't move in a straight line. Instead it bobs and weaves, moves two steps forward and, with luck, only a half step backward. Each time we touched on something that frightened her, Eve regressed. But now instead of retreating to her corner, she simply stopped talking. I told myself this was more than a small step forward, and although my head knew it, my frustration threshold was diminishing.

It was during this phase of the therapy that I went on a vacation to Alaska, where we spent four days sailing on Glacier Bay. Every now and then, we'd hear a deep cracking sound, followed by a rumbling thunderclap as a huge chunk of an iceberg dropped off into the bay. It's a thrilling sight and sound show, but when it's over, the iceberg stands, a new gash visible, a jagged edge that wasn't there before, but still standing, touched but untouched.

Calving, the process is called, a term that fascinated me. Why use the language of birth when something is lost? I wondered when I first saw it. Then as the days passed, I realized that loss isn't the only thing that happens in calving, since along with its new shape, the iceberg takes on a new identity that's visible to those trained to see it. As these thoughts floated half formed through my head, it was clear that Eve, not the iceberg, was preoccupying me. Working with her was like chipping away at an iceberg in which, it had seemed to me, each crack only revealed more ice. Now I realized that there was something more, that each "calving" revealed a new form, the birth of a slightly different Eve. All I had to do was look harder to see it.

I came back to our work with a renewed commitment to keep my impatience in check, to see what wasn't always clearly there to be seen. Unfortunately, Eve didn't return on the same high.

A therapist's comings and goings can be a challenge for patients, although one that I think is often vastly overstated. Indeed, I believe that therapists often encourage their patients to act out each time they go away because we're taught that's what to expect. In my more ungenerous moments about our profession and its rewards, I also think we get a certain amount of narcissistic gratification out of believing we're so central to our patients' lives that they're unable to manage without us and will, as we say to each other, "pay us back" for not being there.

The message we too often send, both verbally and nonverbally, therefore, is: I expect you to be upset and angry. We invite them to talk about it, to tell us how they feel; we assure them that anything they say is okay. And as with a child, if you expect untoward or regressive behavior, you'll get it. It takes a wise patient with a solid adult sense of self to be able to say, as one said to me years ago, "Why should I act like a child? Will it get you to stay?"

29

Certainly, most patients will miss their therapist when they're gone, since it isn't easy when the work is disrupted, whether for other professional obligations the therapist may have or a vacation. And it's useful to talk about those feelings both before and after the separation. But something different happens when that conversation takes place in the context of a therapist's attitude that says "I know this is hard for you but, as you already know, life's not always easy, or even fair."

All this is hindsight, however. I was too new at being a therapist during the time when I was seeing Eve to understand fully how complicit we can be in our patients' regressive behavior. Even if I had known, however, Eve clearly was one of those patients whose ability to connect was fragile enough so that any break in our contact left her feeling abandoned and affirmed for her what she thought she knew: no one could be trusted to be there for her consistently. Everyone would leave, metaphorically, as her parents in their alcoholic haze had, or physically, as I did.

At our first meeting after I came back, therefore, Eve announced that she wanted to reduce our sessions to once a week and refused to discuss it, saying only that she was too busy at work to come more often. I knew this wasn't true and that it wasn't a good idea, that she needed our twice-weekly sessions to sustain her connection with me. By coming once a week she could more easily put me and our work into a compartment she didn't have to open until the next session. But that, of course, was exactly her point. She needed the distance to protect herself from the pain of my comings and goings. But why now? I reminded her that I'd gone away before, that she knew by now that I'd always come back, and asked why this time was different. She shrugged and changed the subject.

The session proceeded fitfully while I tried to figure out what to do. Should I insist we put off any decision until she was willing to talk about it? Was my focus on the pathology underlying her behavior disabling me from seeing something positive here? I decided, finally, that this wasn't only a regressive act but also an attempt at mastery, her way of asserting herself, of feeling less dependent. I knew it was premature, but I hoped something would be gained if she could feel less powerless in the relationship. So we settled on a single hour with my promise that we could revisit the decision should she wish to do so.

The weeks flowed one into the other. We neither progressed nor regressed, a common periodic state in any therapy as patients try to internalize and consolidate the gains they've made. Eve still wanted to "come into the big chair," and we still did that at the end of every hour, although for shorter and shorter periods.

Outside the therapy sessions, however, her life was changing, not in large dramatic gestures, but in small incremental ones. She accepted new clients, allowing her business to grow beyond the one-woman show it had been for so long. She made a friend, the first since high school, with whom she went to an occasional movie or concert. She reported these events matter-of-factly, as if she didn't want me to make too much of them. Then for the first time an hour went by when she didn't ask to sit with me. Neither of us said anything, but in that nonverbal way that two people can share, we both noted it as a landmark event.

The following week she announced that she wanted to resume meeting twice a week. When I asked what brought the change, she said simply, "I'm ready."

"For what?"

"I don't know. Why do I always have to know?"

"Because I think you do know and it's important for us to talk about what happened then and what's going on now."

She shifted around in the chair, her struggle with whether to retreat to her infantile position or speak from her strength written in both her face and body posture. Finally, as if a dam inside gave way, she began to talk about how frightened she had been when I left on my vacation. I had never seen her shed a tear, but now she wept as she recounted her dreams of that time, dreams in which I was lost or drowning or orbiting in space, unable to find my way back to safety; dreams in which she herself was lost or held captive in a forest or locked in a room from which there was no escape.

Once started, it was as if she couldn't stop. For weeks she wept, she raged, she talked. Much of the time I just held her and listened. What was there to say?

She talked about how frightening it was to live in her parents' house, about the beatings she got from her mother, sometimes with her fists, more often with anything that came to her hand, a brush, a pot, an ashtray. "You can't even imagine what it's like, Lillian, never to know what's going to come at you."

I squirmed inwardly. Not only could I imagine it, I'd been there, although not with as much brutality as Eve described. My mother used only her hands and words, ugly bitter words that fell from her mouth and scarred my soul as deeply as her fists racked my body. Talk about countertransference! My throat clenched with the effort to stem the tears that filled my eyes. I didn't know whether I was crying for Eve, for me, or for every child who has ever been abused.

These are sobering moments for a therapist, reminders that our peace with our own past may be more fragile than we know. As I struggled to control the emotions that swept over me, I wanted to tell Eve that it took no imagination to know what she'd suffered. But to speak the words would violate everything I had been taught about never revealing anything about myself to a patient. I wrestled with myself: Do I follow that injunction or go with my heart? Would it comfort Eve to know that I didn't just understand her experience from a distance, that it was mine as well? I had no idea and nothing to rely on for the answer.

The "correct" response to her remark, I knew, was to "analyze the transference," which meant asking her to speak about her fantasies about me and my life. I was caught: I didn't dare speak what I was thinking, and I couldn't imagine trivializing what she was experiencing by asking her to deal with her transference fantasies, which in that moment seemed irrelevant. Today I would make a different choice, one that would let a patient know she wasn't alone. Then I kept silent.

As the weeks passed and the wall she had erected against both feeling and memory continued to crumble, she was able to speak about her father's forays into her bedroom, about how, at six, she was inducted into the art of manual stimulation and within a year into fellatio. I've had many patients who were abused sexually and always it plays havoc with both the child and the woman. But I also know that in at least some of those cases, the woman understands that, horrible as the experience was, the child got something out of it — some special attention, small gifts to make her feel loved, some tenderness in a family where there was little, something that told her she was important, had a special place in the world. "He called me *princess*" was the way one patient put it.

I don't mean to suggest that a child is ever at fault, that this most heinous kind of abuse is ever forgivable, or that whatever she might have gained, the child didn't also hate what was happening. But it's worth noting that, like all human behavior this, too, can be complicated and that a therapist must listen carefully to what women say about their guilt before jumping to reassuring words that can seem empty to the patient.

With Eve, however, there was no suggestion of any gain for her. It was a brutal, wordless exploitation, not a hint of caring by a man who used his child's body and left her curled up in her bed wishing she could die before the next time. He never actually penetrated her, but it was rape, nevertheless — the rape of her body, her mind, her innocence, her belief in her own humanity.

She tried to tell her mother who brushed her off and returned to her drink. Desperate, she ran away and was picked up by the police to whom she told her story. They called her parents, who explained that Eve was a troubled child and an habitual liar. The police sent her home to more beatings and more sexual abuse.

Despite her efforts to rescue herself, she could never fully believe that she wasn't somehow at fault, even if only by what she called her *female presence* in the household. The words struck me: *female presence*. It isn't as if I hadn't thought before that the clothes she wore were designed to hide her sexuality — a capacious coat under which were dark, unattractive clothes that were far to big for her small frame, all of it topped off by the white hat that hid her face. But now here was the evidence; her own words opened the door. "I've always wondered why you try so hard to make yourself so unattractive. You must have wanted to do whatever possible to hide yourself from him, and now from other men."

Startled, she sat quietly for a while, then said teasingly, "You think you're pretty smart, don't you?"

Two weeks later the coat was replaced by a handsome leather jacket. I remarked that I liked how she looked in it. She replied that she'd seen me on the street wearing such a jacket and had wanted one since then. I asked why she hadn't bought it before.

"I guess I wasn't ready."

"Meaning what?"

"You know, Lillian," she exclaimed in exasperation, "there's more than one kind of closet."

Change came quickly after that as week by week she added something new — clothes that mimicked the kind I wore as she sought both to fortify her identification with me and to reclaim her sexuality, a stylish haircut, some makeup, lipstick, eye-liner, a faint blush on her cheeks, none of which she'd ever worn before. But the white hat, jammed low on her head, persisted. Then one day it disappeared, signaling the way no words could that the main part of our work was finished.

A year later I watched Eve walk out the door, tearful at having to part but with her head held high. I stood at the window, my eyes following her small figure cross the street and climb into her car, my heart filled with the same mix of pride and sadness I felt when I saw my daughter off to college. I knew I'd see Eve again; we had agreed that she could come back for what she called a *tune-up* whenever she wanted to. But just as I understood on the day my daughter left that our lives would never be the same again, so I knew that, no matter how many hellos and good-byes Eve and I might have in the future, nothing to come would match the intensity of this moment or the power and importance of the relationship we'd shared.

The Man with the Beautiful Voice

The great insight, the long-forgotten memory, the trans-formative "aha" experience make good movie fare, but the heart of therapy, its nuts and bolts, is in the commonplace, in a person's response to the simplest and most unremarkable events. An experienced therapist, therefore, usually can tell a lot about a patient from the way the initial phone call and request for an appointment plays itself out. Does the person seem overly deferential in asking to speak to "the doctor"? Or after listening to my message, delivered in my most professional tones, does the voice at the other end say cheerily, "Hey, Lillian, this is . . . ?" Both send cues, although very different ones, about how each of these people will relate to me as a therapist and an authority figure.

Similarly, if, when I return the call, a person begins to tell me her life story seconds after she asks for an appointment, I know this is someone whose need is great and who has, what we call in the trade, *boundary problems*. If someone asks what kind of therapy I do and no matter how many questions I answer still has one more, I expect to meet a patient who's untrusting and controlling.

Bruce Marins's richly timbered voice on my answering machine caught and held my attention immediately, but it took several rounds of phone tag before we spoke one evening. Meanwhile the messages he left, his wit, when on the third try we still hadn't connected, suggested to me a man of considerable humor and intellect, one who was confident of his ability to charm and knew how to use his beautiful voice as an instrument of seduction.

I was intrigued. At the time I had what felt like more than my fair share of patients who came each week to do what I think of as *storytelling*, a repetitive recitation of their frustrations, sometimes a new story, sometimes an old one, but always the same themes and conflicts, which they seemed incapable of resolving. Everyone has such patients, and each of us finds her own way to deal with them, some more easily than others. But I've never met a therapist who doesn't know what it's like to look at the clock thinking surely this hour will soon be over, only to find that there are still forty minutes left. One colleague recently confided, "In my mind I split the hour up into ten-minute segments and try not to look at the clock until I'm pretty sure ten minutes have gone by."

"Does it work?"

She replied with a laugh, "Only if the purpose is to find out just how long ten minutes can be."

It's in this context that Bruce Marins presented himself as a welcome diversion. From our telephone contacts, I assumed that I'd find myself in the presence of a man with a fairly heavy dose of narcissism, but I'd worked well with such men and looked forward to the challenge. I also knew that I'd have to watch my countertransference, which already was evident in the way he'd insinuated himself into my thoughts. My warning to myself notwithstanding, I found myself with images of a tall, dark, handsome man, someone whose appearance would match his marvelous voice, as I waited with a frisson of pleasant anticipation for the bell to signal his arrival for his first appointment.

When I opened the door that connects my office to the waiting room, I wasn't conscious of the habitual welcoming smile on my face. I only realized it was there after I felt it slip away when I beheld the man before me and heard the same melodious voice say, "I wiped that smile off your face pretty fast, didn't I?" Only this time the seduction was gone, replaced by an edge of mockery,

I stood in the doorway, stopped in mid-stride both by his words and the incongruity between what I had imagined and the man who stood in the middle of the small waiting room, his back bent over his crutches, his lower body seeming atrophied, and his legs encased in braces from hip to foot. We stared at each other, he with a mocking smile, I beginning to feel the heat of anger at what felt like a deliberate setup.

It wasn't a lack of words that kept me silent for a moment or two. My brain swam with thoughts, but I needed time to sort them out and decide which would be best to speak. I could acknowledge my surprise, but he already knew that, as his remark told me, and I was virtually certain he had planned it that way. I could play it safe by ignoring his comment and welcoming him into the office while I waited to see where he'd go from there. But it's not a mode that comes naturally to me, and I'd learned long ago that, especially in such difficult situations, I'm most effective when I'm most authentic. Finally, I did what felt genuine and confronted the situation head-on. "Do you always set people up like that or did you reserve that just for me?"

He laughed, an angry challenging sound, and said, "I see this is going to be fun."

"Why don't we go in and get started then," I said.

"Seems to me we already have," he replied.

Another point for you, I thought, but I just smiled and said, "Yes, you're right, so let's sit down and be comfortable."

With a nod he moved toward the door, his head bent, his shoulders hunched over the crutches with which he pulled his body along, each step of his withered legs seeming to be an exercise in will. As I watched his slow progress, I was struck by the sharp contrast between the breadth of his well-muscled upper torso and the puny look of the lower half of his body. Finally, his crutches laid carefully on the floor beside him, he sank into the chair I indicated and scanned my face intently as if to see what he could read there.

We sat quietly taking each other's measure. He held my gaze with an enigmatic smile, and I knew that if I didn't speak first we would end up in a power struggle that was a lose-lose proposition for both of us. So I plunged in. "I'm sure you remember the question I asked when we were in the waiting room, and I wonder if you'd care to answer it now?"

"Don't you want to know something about me first? Every other shrink I've ever seen started with some mealymouthed 'Tell me about yourself.'"

I said I certainly did need to know a lot about him if we were to work together, but that he was right when he said we'd already started something, and it might be best if we tried to finish that first.

"So what do you think we started?" he asked belligerently.

"Well, as I said, I think you set me up to be surprised by your handicap . . ."

He interrupted sharply, "Dammit, don't use euphemisms with me. I'm a cripple. Do you think you can say the word, or are we going to have to dance around it so you don't have to be uncomfortable? Anyway, what would you have wanted me to do, announce on the phone that I'm a fucking cripple so you could get used to it. That's your problem, not mine."

He's right, I thought; what could he have done? One answer, of course, was that he didn't have to set out deliberately to seduce me. But then that, too, is a part of him, just as is his crippled body, and there's no reason why that part should have gone into hiding. The reality I wasn't eager to look at, however, is that his refusal to hide his infirmity behind the usual polite civilities forced me into a confrontation with my discomfort in his presence, which until then I'd been able to displace into anger at his behavior.

I'd never had such close contact with a person who was so severely disabled. I was afraid I wouldn't have the right words, or maybe even the right thoughts. But even as I explained my discomfort to myself, I knew it was more than that. In truth, my feelings were something akin to those I've had when seeing a homeless person on the street, a kind of fascination and revulsion at the same time — a sense of outrage that, in the wealthiest nation in the world, people are forced to live on the street, coupled with a wish to turn away, to block it all out of consciousness so as not to have to deal with the morass of guilt, anger, and helplessness the sight stirs.

Talk about countertransference issues to try a therapist's soul. As I looked into Bruce's eyes, I knew that this therapy would be an ongoing confrontation with myself — yet another moment when I was reminded that the therapeutic enterprise can be as much a learning experience for the therapist as for the patient.

I never before thought much about my response to the disabled. I had all the politically correct words at my command, of course, and I could even summon up what I thought were the "right" feelings. But what I felt in the first shock of seeing Bruce wasn't any of those more acceptably civilized responses. My immediate impulse was to turn away, to shield my eyes, to turn them to something less . . . less what? I can barely allow myself to think the word, let alone say it . . . less repugnant.

I wasn't without sympathy for the man who sat before me. But, angry as it made me then, I would learn that Bruce was right in rejecting that sympathy as patronizing, a way of dealing with my own guilt and discomfort and a way of categorizing him, *a disabled person*, someone to feel sorry for because he isn't like the rest of us, a man but not quite a man.

Examining these feelings, however, was for another time. In the moment I had to respond. So after wrestling with myself for a few seconds, I replied, "You're right, that *is* my problem, and I'll deal with it. But how we handle this fact of your life and whether we allow it to dominate our relationship and disable our work is *our* problem."

His body language softened and some of the tension seeped out of the room. "At least you didn't throw it all back into my lap."

I laughed. "I guess that means you have some hope for me."

He relented, grudgingly allowed as how I deserved an answer to my question, and acknowledged that he had set me up. "It was important to me to see how you'd react because I get so damn much phoniness coming my way, people pretending they don't see what they see. I didn't want to have to go through that with another shrink who's always tiptoeing around. But if you don't mind, right now I'd like to talk about something else."

I thanked him for his honesty and asked what was on his mind, assuming that some immediately pressing problem had brought him into therapy. But in fact there was no "something else." I don't mean that he didn't have problems and conflicts that needed resolution, but so many of them stemmed from his being crippled that this *became* the central fact of his life and of the therapy we would do together.

Bruce Marins had the misfortune of lying in his mother's womb at the time when doctors discovered that Thalidomide, a relatively new drug in this country then, would cure the morning sickness that plagues so many women, his mother included, in the early months of their pregnancy. Eight months after his mother swallowed the pills her doctor prescribed, Bruce was born with both legs deformed, one of the many thousands of children who would become known collectively as Thalidomide babies, some whose bodies were disfigured so grotesquely that any semblance of a normal life was forever closed to them.

Every parent experiences some measure of irrational guilt (What did I do wrong?) when a child is born with even a small defect. But the parents of Thalidomide babies, especially their mothers, bear a special burden of guilt and blame because they *know* what went wrong and are stuck with the *should have, would have, could have* scenario that nearly inevitably follows such a tragedy. No matter how often a woman may tell herself that she was following doctor's orders, she'll probably never fully escape the fact that she put the pills in her mouth.

Over the years I've treated some families of these children and have seen firsthand the psychological devastation the tragedy wrought. Fathers blaming mothers, mothers blaming themselves; couples unable to get past the guilt, blame, shame, and rage. I've seen a father turn away from a child because "looking at her hurts too much"; another whose rage at his wife for taking the pills, and at God for allowing his son to live split the family asunder. I've worked with mothers who were so oppressed by guilt they contemplated suicide, and others so depressed that all light had seeped from their world. But Bruce was my first personal contact with an adult who was the victim of that notorious pill.

When I was able to get past my initial response, I saw a man whose dark curly hair, worn fashionably long and well coiffed, made an appealing frame for his strong, square, olive-complexioned face. Intelligence radiated from his blue-green eyes, which were so startlingly bright that I thought they must be the product of colored contact lenses. Not the beautiful prince of my imagination, but a man who could have been very attractive if anger didn't mark every line of his face. He was impeccably dressed in an expensive charcoal-colored suit, light blue shirt, its sleeves fastened by silver cuff links, and a lightly patterned deep red tie that matched the gemstone adorning the links. Everything about his appearance bespoke success, yet he oozed an air of anger that made me wonder how he got there.

From the time he was a small child, he reported, he had been good with both words and images and spent many hours making up stories and drawing pictures to illustrate them. In adulthood, he got started in the advertising business because it was the best job offered to him after college. Now, fourteen years later, he was the West Coast creative director of a well-known ad agency. He still occasionally tried his hand at writing something more serious than advertising copy, but mostly he spent his very limited spare time painting, usually portraits. I listened carefully and admiringly as he laid out both his talents and his successes and finally remarked in what I thought was a warmly supportive way, "That's quite a list of accomplishments."

"Why," he snapped back instantly, "because I'm a cripple?"

I sighed. "Is there anything I might have said that wouldn't have generated that response?"

"Not until I'm certain that's not the unspoken message."

Was it? My immediate impulse was to say "No, that's not it; I'm genuinely impressed." Which may have been true. But when I recalled my internal response when I first saw him, I knew it wasn't the only truth.

I didn't have to figure it out right then because we were close to the end of the hour and, as is my wont in a first session, I suggested that we stop and talk about how he felt about what went on and whether he wanted to come back. He wasn't sure, he said; he thought I was "smart enough" but was uncertain whether I had "the stomach" for dealing with him.

"Why, because you're crippled?"

"Okay, so you proved you can say *the word*, but it doesn't tell me a damn thing about whether I can trust you. So the answer is yes, because I'm a cripple and also because I'm a hard-ass son of a bitch."

I sighed, thinking how attractive his quick wit and keen intelligence could have made him if he didn't use them like a sword. And I wondered for a moment whether I really wanted to take up the challenge he presented. I already had a couple of patients who were expert at denigrating everything I said and finding inventive ways to defeat our work. Did I really need another one? But inspite of his truculence, something about him caught and held me.

Who knows what mix of emotion and chemistry went into my emotional response to him? Maybe it was, as he feared, pity; maybe it was respect for his struggle; maybe he touched the place inside me that had been a lonely child; maybe I identified with his anger and understood, as I had learned in my own life, that it was partly motivated by fear that a disabling depression lurked underneath it; maybe I sensed that below the surface lived a man I could really like; maybe I knew he had something to teach me about myself; maybe all of the above and more I couldn't know then. I knew only that I didn't want him to walk away. So I said as gently as I knew how, "That's certainly the side you've shown me today, but I also see a man who's dug himself into a hole and covered it up with rage so neither he nor anyone else would have to face his vulnerabilities."

At that his arm flung out in a gesture as if to wave me away, then he leaned down, grabbed his crutches, pulled himself upright, and made his painful way out of the room, calling back over his shoulder, "I'll call you."

I watched him leave, feeling let down and angry with myself. I wasn't surprised that he was upset, but I had bet that he was strong enough so that whatever anxiety my observation raised would be offset by the reassurance I offered that he was seen and understood. Clearly I'd lost the bet.

Was it too much, too soon? So much of therapy is in the timing, and I know I have a tendency sometimes to move too fast. The same comment or interpretation that's helpful when a patient is ready can be met with resistance when he's not. A psychiatrist I saw as a patient a few years ago remarked, when we were ending his therapy, that he had learned a lot about psychotherapy from our work together and that he was much more likely to respond openly to a patient than he had been before. But there were times, he said, when he thought I "shoot from the hip," and although he could see that it worked most of the time, he wondered about the times when it must have been "disastrous."

I thought about his words after Bruce left and wondered if this was one of those disasters he foresaw. I hated the thought. It wasn't just my ego at stake, although I certainly didn't feel good to think I'd blundered. I was hooked by the challenge Bruce presented, by what I could learn from him, and by my long-standing interest in resilience. I was, at the time, in the middle of a research project in which I was interviewing adults who had transcended seriously difficult childhoods. I had by then learned a good deal about what enables some people to surmount early traumatic experiences while others are felled by them. I was impressed with how Bruce had managed to overcome his infirmity in the professional world, and my clinical intuition told me he was ready to take the next step into his internal world. All I had to do was find the key. But first he had to decide to come back, and there was nothing to do now but wait.

Three days later the wait was over. Bruce left a message saying he wanted another appointment but would prefer not to wait a week. Fortunately I had a cancellation the next day and called back to offer him the hour.

Even before he sat down, he informed me that he had checked me out on Nexis, that he found my "résumé very impressive," and that he had no idea that I was "so important." In the few days since I'd seen him he'd also read one of my books, *Quiet Rage*, which he pronounced "very smart." He talked for a couple of minutes about the book and about what rage can do when it has been silenced, then with a grin, the first I'd seen, concluded, "From the title I figured you might be talking about people like me, but then I guess you don't think my rage is so quiet, do you?"

I laughed, pleased with this indication of self-awareness, but before I could say anything, he leaned forward, his eyes holding mine and explained that he'd seen three or four therapists before, never for more than a few visits, because none of them was "much of a brain" and "even when they talked, they never had anything interesting to say." After checking me out he decided I was "smart enough to be worth a try." Nothing about our first hour, nothing about his feelings when he fled from the room. All in all, not a ringing endorsement, but a beginning.

In the weeks and months that followed we examined his nighttime dreams, his daytime fantasies, his life in the present, and his past experiences in the family and the world outside. His was a middle-class family, financially comfortable enough to, as he said bitterly, "give their kids everything they needed and more, I mean, everything but what a kid really needs." He had one brother, Pete, three years younger than he, a child who was conceived "to make up for them having me. How the hell can anybody expect a little kid to do that?" he asked, his voice dripping with rancor, as he reflected on Pete's lifetime of failure.

His father, he recalled, "could never really look at me," and he was convinced that he wished Bruce had died so he wouldn't have to deal with having a crippled son. Of his mother he said, "As far back as I can remember, she'd look at me with blank eyes, like she couldn't stand to really see me. Neither of them ever saw anything but the cripple they created."

As angry as he was with his father it was easier than with his mother because "at least I knew what he wanted: a son who would be the athlete he could be proud of. But my mother just walked around like in a fog. You never knew what the hell would make it okay for her, and believe me I tried, for years I tried." He told of the time when he was twelve and spent days writing and illustrating a story, which he made into a book to give to his mother on Mother's Day. "I thought for sure it would make her happy for a minute, but all she did was look at it and cry."

Despite his efforts to speak calmly, his pain and sadness enveloped both of us, and I had to struggle to keep my feelings in check and hold back tears. Not that I think there's anything wrong with allowing a patient to see me as human in that way, but because I knew that Bruce would see any display of feeling as born in pity rather than in empathy and identity, and it would bring down his wrath. So I made what I thought was an obvious comment. "You spent so much of your life trying to make it okay for your mother, it's no wonder you were worried about having to take care of me."

He looked startled, his face reddening as he fought to contain the feelings that rose up in him. He wasn't ready yet to let me see the hurt too clearly, nor could he risk a confrontation with the needy child inside him. What if he let the guard down and found out I was no different from the rest? So he threw me a sidewise glance and said gruffly, "Yeah, I said you were smart."

I noted, not for the first time, how much being smart meant to Bruce, how important it was to him to believe I was not just smart but smarter than others. It's not unusual for patients, especially those who lean toward narcissism, to need to believe their therapist is the smartest of all. But it was something deeper for Bruce who, it was clear from the outset, was saved from disaster by the gifts with which he was born. And being smart was high among them. Like other children who transcend early difficulties, he made the most of what he had, using his artistic talent and intelligence to gain success and admiration, first in school, then on the job where, unlike in his family, some people at least could see beyond his crippled body.

But none of his successes cooled his angry distrust of the people around him. When a child grows up, as Bruce did, with parents who see him as a cross to bear, he has two options. The most dysfunctional one is to keep knocking on the door that's closed to him, to make winning their love and approval the cornerstone of his childhood. The other is to make an emotional separation from them long before any child should have to do so and try to compensate with whatever positive experiences and relationships he can find. It's Bruce's strength that he did the latter. But to accomplish this difficult psychological task, he bottled up his need for companionship, love, warmth, another's touch, and corked it with his anger.

I had myself felt the heat of his anger, and I knew how hard it was to deal with his relentless testing. Time and again, I came up against the barriers he erected to frustrate any approach I made, and I often marveled at how skillful he was at keeping me at bay. I was certain, therefore, that, consciously or not, he had engineered the failure of at least some of his relationships. His rageful, distrusting behavior, designed to protect himself from the pain of rejection, practically assured the very outcome he feared.

His wariness reached its height around women, with whom he had no relationships at all, neither friendship nor sex. Twice, once in college and once soon after he got his first job, he met a woman who "seemed different." But he saw deceit, pity, and rejection wherever he turned and the budding friendships ended "in disaster." In his thirty-six years his only non-commercial sexual encounter was with a high school classmate who, he said, "came on to me so she could brag about doing it with the crip." Since then, when he needed sexual release and masturbation didn't satisfy, he sought out a prostitute who did what he wanted "with no pity and no questions asked."

His relationships weren't much better with men than with women. He became friendly with a couple of men at college with whom he studied occasionally, but soon bowed out of any social activities because he "felt like a drag on them." On the job he did somewhat better than in his personal life, largely because he had no choice but to find some way to relate amicably, or at least not disruptively. He managed dealing with workmates by keeping a cool distance and by, he said with a caustic jab at himself, "my rapier wit." He liked his boss, an older man who recognized and nourished his talent and whom he described as "the closest thing to a father I'll ever have." But despite the obvious attachment, except for the social events required by the business, he never allowed the relationship to go beyond the office door. When I asked why, he replied sourly, "Work's one thing, but nobody wants a cripple hanging around and spoiling the party."

By then, we had been working together for well over a year. I can't say we'd established a close rapport, but he wasn't always angry, he no longer denigrated everything I said, and we could occasionally engage in the kind of wordless communication that can happen when therapist and patient have developed a working alliance. So I said nothing, letting him listen to the echoes of his own words, hoping he'd hear them as I had.

My silence discomfited him, accustomed as he was to jousting with me, and his anger, never too far from the surface, rose. "Dammit, say something."

I shrugged, wordlessly. Finally, he shouted, "You still don't get it, do you? You're sitting there with that smug look thinking it's my problem, but dammit it's not that way. You can be sure he wouldn't want me marrying his daughter."

It was hard to stay cool, hard not to respond with something like "How can you be so sure when you never gave him a chance?" But a voice inside stepped in with a warning that kept me silent.

"What?" he shouted.

I shrugged again, eyebrows raised, palms turned up.

"Christ, you know I hate it when you do that shrink number. What the hell do you want from me?" His hands raked his hair, his face a mask of the most profound weary pain I'd ever seen.

Inside I was in turmoil. I wanted to move to his side, to take his hand, hold his head to my breast, offer him the comfort and love I knew he needed. Outside I sat quietly, cautioning myself to wait to see where he would go. Finally, his eyes brimming with unshed tears, he spoke in a voice quieter and gentler than I'd ever before heard from him. "I know what you want; I don't need you to say the words. But it's so damn hard to give people that chance you're always talking about. I did that with them [referring to his parents] over and over and look what it got me. How do I know who to trust?"

It was a critical moment in his therapy, and I had a decision to make. It seemed to me that the time was right, that he wouldn't retreat from a move, that he was ready for a deeper, more intimate relationship with me than he'd ever had with anyone in his life. But I couldn't be sure whether it was intuition speaking to me or wishful thinking. I wanted to reach out to him as I would to anyone in such pain, to let him know I was moved by the emotional depth of his response. But what if I was wrong? What if it was too much, too soon? What if I awakened his fear and drove him back into his cave?

I can't say I made a reasoned choice, but then I don't think reason is what counts at a time like that. It's that indefinable something we call *clinical intuition* that guides every good therapist in these decisive junctures in a therapy. And mine told me to do what *felt* right and hope it wasn't one of those shoot-from-the-hip moments.

I moved to the hassock that separated our two chairs, reached over, took his hand in both of mine, and said softly, "You knew enough to trust me. Why wouldn't you be able to do that again?"

He looked away but left his hand in place, then struggling to keep his voice steady, replied, "You're paid to be trustworthy."

"Really?" I asked, holding up our joined hands to his view. "Am I paid to do this, too?"

He squeezed my hand and said, "Sorry," a word I wasn't sure I'd ever hear him speak.

This was the beginning. Until now we had nibbled around the edges of his psyche. I saw some change in him, largely in the easier way he could relate to me. On the outside, however, his world remained as closed and isolated as ever. But this hour was a turning point. For the first time in his adult life he moved from emotional isolation to intimacy from which he wasn't impelled to flee. For the first time he believed that someone could see his need and meet it.

Early in our work I had asked to see Bruce's paintings, partly because I've always been interested in art and artists, partly because I thought it might help form a bond between us, and partly because I thought I'd learn something about him that wouldn't be so easily accessible with words. But he was steadfast in his refusal. "I don't show them to anyone; I paint for myself."

A few weeks after the session in which I'd held his hand and some of his defenses crumbled, he arrived with a canvas, which he carried pinned against his body as he maneuvered it and himself into the room. "You wanted to see one of my paintings," he said with no further explanation.

I took it somewhat apprehensively, knowing that this was a gift of trust and that much hung on how I received it. I turned the canvas to me carefully and stood awestruck by its power. It was a portrait of a woman, every line of her body speaking to an agonizingly profound dejection. When I could finally speak, I said exactly what I thought and hoped it was the right thing. "I can't say it's easy to look at, but it's one of the most powerful portraits I've ever seen and an absolutely marvelous painting."

From then on, his paintings became an integral part of the therapy. Every few weeks he brought another one in. Finally, after watching his struggle to get himself and the painting into the office, I asked if he'd like me to drive by his house and pick up a few at a time. "You'd do that? Isn't it against the rules?"

I laughed. "If you don't tell, I won't."

It was another defining moment for him, a statement that I cared enough about him and what was clearly his heart's work to go out of my way to see it. For the next several months we examined the portraits together, appreciated them, criticized them, analyzed them for what they could tell him about himself, his fears, his desires. Far more than his dreams, they held up a mirror to his internal life. His palette was somber, the occasional flash of red or orange serving only to highlight the darkness of the canvas.

Every one of the portraits was stunning, his enormous talent apparent in each stroke of his brush; all were frightening in his vision of his subjects. Over and over he painted his parents, looking, it seemed, for something he could never find. The women were all in some painfully depressive posture; the men cold, hard, often turned away as if to avert their eyes from what they didn't want to see. But it was his self-portraits that were the most striking, gnarled, bent, crippled images of an ugly man whose eyes were filled with angry self-loathing.

It was chilling to see his vision of himself, to realize that this was not far off from what I had seen when we first met. Now, two-plus years later, these portraits no longer looked like the man I knew. Was it I who had changed? Or did he really look different? We hadn't talked about his being crippled for a long time, and I was somewhat anxious about raising the issue now, fearful perhaps that I'd find out that I still hadn't passed the test. Finally, I gulped one day and took the plunge. "These don't look like you anymore, and I wonder whether you think it's because I've changed, you have, or we both have?"

He thought about that for a minute, then in a voice so tender it overwhelmed me, "I don't know about me, but I know you have." Then returning to the more bantering style that marked our relationship, "Not a cringe in sight, not even one you thought I wouldn't notice."

"Thank you," I replied, not trying to hide how deeply his words moved me. "But you haven't looked very hard, either inside yourself or in the mirror, if you think you haven't changed, too."

A few months later he brought in a new piece, a self-portrait of a man who was crippled but not ugly, the first painting that actually resembled him. Even the colors were different, the same tones but lighter hues, reflecting a brighter, more hopeful view of the world.

We stood looking at it together, tears streaking both our faces. I turned and hugged him; he wrapped his arms, still holding his crutches, around me and held on tight. We didn't need to say it; we knew our work was done. We continued to see each other for several more months while we processed where we had come from and where we were now. But except for saying goodbye, the active work of therapy was over.

I don't mean he became a different person. Despite the public press and our wish that we could do it, therapy doesn't transform anyone. We leave therapy changed only in that we have a better understanding of who we are and how to deal with the troubled and troubling parts of ourselves. But *knowing* itself, important though it may be, is not enough to enable us to live life more productively. It's what we *do* with the knowledge, how we manage to live with the scars life inevitably leaves, that counts. For no matter how long we're in therapy, no matter how much we learn there, old scars will bleed when picked and new issues will arise to push us back into old responses. A successful therapy leaves us enabled to deal with both in a new and more fruitful way.

So it was with Bruce Marins, who left therapy as physically crippled as he was on the day he walked in. He still faced a world that turned away; his parents still couldn't look at him without pain and guilt; the wounds of a lifetime, although scarred over, could still bleed when scratched. But he no longer allowed those realities to define him and control his life. With a new ability to trust, he could let go of some of the anger and let some people come close.

Three years after our last session, Bruce called to tell me there would be a showing of his work at a San Francisco gallery. A year after that I was invited to his wedding.

The Woman Who Wasn't

They came into my office together, referred by one of her colleagues. He was a tall man in his early thirties, his ill-fitting clothes rumpled, his early youthful slimness slipping away behind too much food and too little exercise. Still, with his gray wide-set eyes, dark curly hair, and long, well-proportioned face, it was a look I might have found attractive. But there was something about him that put me off, something loose, as if all the parts didn't quite hold together, and squishy, as if I poked my finger into his middle, I'd leave a dent like in the Pillsbury Doughboy.

She was short and slightly plump, her brown eyes set close together in a round face framed by nondescript brown hair that looked as if it had been molded in place. Her clothes fit like a second skin, with not even a wrinkle to suggest that they had been worn at work all day. A woman whose looks were so ordinary that, except for the uncommon neatness, I wouldn't have given her a passing glance if she were sitting across from me on a bus.

Bonnie Paulsen and Jerry Stillman. At first sight they seemed like an odd couple. Where he was casually and loosely put together, she was held together so tightly that I thought she might be corseted, even though it was long past the era when women wore those ungodly contraptions. Where he smiled ingratiatingly, she remained intensely serious, her expression on the edge of a disapproving frown. Where he had a hard time meeting my eye, her unblinking stare unsettled me. They both exhibited the kind of discomfort that's common on a first visit, but she was filled with a speedy tension that dominated the air around her.

They were both mid-level executives working for different companies but in related fields. They met when their paths crossed at work, had been together for three years, and had come into couples therapy to "figure out some things" about their relationship. Even before they spoke, everything about the way they looked and presented themselves told me that she was the controlling partner. So it wasn't a surprise when her voice dominated the hour and refused to let go.

I didn't object because her story fascinated me and she clearly needed to tell it. She was an abandoned infant, "thrown away," is the way she put it, when she was just a few hours old. She spent the first seven months of her life in a foster home, after which she was adopted by a family and taken to a small northeastern city where she grew up, the only child in a comfortable middle-class home with extended family — grandparents, aunts, uncles, cousins — all living nearby.

Although her adoptive parents were decent people who provided well for her, she was deeply resentful of her mother who, she believed, spent her life mourning her inability to have "her own flesh-and-blood child." The extended family was close and Bonnie spent a lot of time in its midst, but she never felt at one with any of them. They were all tall, slim, blond, and blue-eyed; she was short, round, dark, and brown-eyed. This difference, the knowledge that she didn't look like anyone around her, loomed large in her sense of alienation from the family. "They were like golden people," she recalled with bitterness. "I felt like I was the brown chick, the sport or the accident among all the golden ones. Everyone else looked like someone; it seemed like I was the only one in the world who didn't look like anybody else."

She claimed to remember the day she was taken from her foster home and described the room in which she met her adoptive parents as big, with green walls and a table in the center. She recounted a recurrent vision, not a dream she insisted, in which she saw herself lying on her back in this green room, a bright light shining down while strangers prodded and poked her. That, she said, was the last time she ever cried. And also the last time she dared to sleep with her eyes closed.

I knew it was possible to sleep with eyes wide open, but I'd never met anyone before who did it, and I wasn't sure what to believe. But before I could ask a question, Jerry stepped in (the only time he took the initiative to speak) and affirmed her story. "It's really weird; I never saw anything like it," he remarked, shaking his head as if he still found it unnerving. "At first I didn't think she was really asleep, like maybe she was pretending or something. But it's true; she never closes her eyes, even when she's sound asleep."

As Bonnie continued her story, I was struck by the straight-faced and conspicuously low affect with which she recounted the difficult experiences of her early years. Consequently, my own inner response, while sympathetic, was more intellectual than emotional. It felt as if her dulled affect had rubbed off on me, as if I had unconsciously absorbed her emotional state and had for the moment made it my own.

It's not an uncommon countertransference phenomenon for a therapist to mimic the feeling state of a patient in this way. If the therapist can stay on top of her feelings and understand their source, she can learn a lot both about herself and her patient. So I noted my reaction and knew I'd be grappling with it later.

But now the hour was coming to an end, and I was left to wonder what these two really wanted from me. They had come in together saying they wanted couples therapy, yet not a word had been spoken about the issues that concerned them. I remarked about that and wondered aloud if they thought some of the difficult past Bonnie recounted was making itself felt in their relationship. My suggestion was met with a blank silence until Bonnie finally said simply, "I don't know." I asked if they could at least give me some idea of the problems they wanted to work on. Bonnie said they'd think about it; Jerry remained silent. I turned to him and asked if there was something he wanted to add. Smiling agreeably, he replied, "No, not really."

I didn't feel much like smiling back. Instead, I found myself struggling to hold my impatience in check while reminding myself that it's not always a negative in the therapeutic encounter. For I've learned over the years that my impatience is both my strength and my weakness as a therapist — weakness because I sometimes expect too much, too soon; strength because I don't let people just drift along for years. The problem is knowing when it serves me and my patient well and when it doesn't.

I closed the door behind them with a sigh of relief, but my mind kept returning to them over the next day or two as I tried to sort out my feelings about the hour we'd spent together. I found myself caught between going over the details Bonnie had presented and my persistent internal image of a woman encased in a crust, something like a chicken baked in clay that you have to shatter with a mallet when you want to get at the meat.

Despite the vague uneasiness that hovered over my thoughts, Bonnie's story and the way she told it was unusual enough to present an irresistible challenge, the kind every therapist looks for to break the ordinary predictability of so much of what we hear in our consulting rooms. I had no doubt that this would be a difficult therapy, but I was confident enough in my therapeutic skills (some might call it arrogant) to believe I could break through the tough crust I'd witnessed and help Bonnie find a fuller life than she had been capable of until then.

The day before our next scheduled session, Bonnie called to say they had decided she should do some individual therapy rather than couples work. I was puzzled: "What brought this on? How did Jerry feel about the change in direction?"

The session we had, she said, convinced her that she needed to deal with her past, although she wasn't quite sure what that meant. As for Jerry, he was "a hundred percent behind the plan." I wondered if Jerry would ever be anything but "a hundred percent behind" any plan Bonnie devised. Still, I thought I ought to speak with him directly and suggested that they come in together the next day when we could talk about it.

"That's really not necessary," she assured me. "It was a hard decision for me and I really want to get going. Maybe you could just talk to him right now." At her request he picked up the phone but, no matter how I phrased my questions, he repeated almost verbatim everything she said.

It was clear: Bonnie would run the show and talking to Jerry face-to-face wouldn't change the outcome. I had a decision to make quickly: Do I send them away, insist on seeing them together one more time, or accede to her terms? Something was making me edgy, some sense that something was wrong with the way this was taking shape. Was this uneasiness telling me something I ought to heed, or was I being a bit paranoid?

It's almost axiomatic that once you've seen a couple together it's unwise (some say never) to agree to see one of them for individual therapy. By and large it's not a bad principle to hold to because, even when one member of the couple assures you that it's just what he wants, there are almost always complications, some difficult but manageable, others insurmountable. And I've had reason in the past to rue the day I broke the rule.

A few years ago, for example, I saw a couple I'll call Katherine and Richard; she was a psychologist, he an attorney. Both were discontented with the relationship, she because he was distant and preoccupied, he because he couldn't understand what she wanted and was angry about what he called their "impoverished sexual relationship." She was determined to mend the marriage; he wasn't sure whether he wanted to continue it. She had done a fair amount of individual therapy; he had never been in a therapist's office before. Early in our work together, I suggested that he might do well with some individual therapy. He agreed and over the next several months saw two different therapists, each for two or three visits, then quit because they weren't "right."

After about a year of couples therapy, it seemed to me that we couldn't go much further until he dealt with his own issues and conflicts. They thought about it, then came to their next session and announced that they would agree to stop the couples therapy only if I would consent to see him individually. I demurred, explaining that it was risky, that if, in the end, it turned out he really wanted out of the marriage, I would have to honor that, and she would feel betrayed by both of us.

None of my arguments moved them. He argued that it was the only course that made sense, since he had trouble working with anyone else and already liked and respected me. She insisted that, as a psychologist in clinical practice, she understood the risks, knew that I would have to be acting in the best interest of my patient as I understood that, and that it would be ludicrous for her to hold me accountable for the end of what was already a troubled marriage. After several weeks of such discussion, I finally agreed to see him alone.

Six months into the therapy he met and fell in love with another woman; a few months later he told Katherine he wanted a divorce. She responded by blaming me and sent a letter so vitriolic, so filled with rage at my betrayal that remembering it now, years later, makes me wince.

I played that old script over in my mind and told myself to beware. But it wasn't the same. I hadn't done therapy with Bonnie and Jerry; we'd had only a single consultation session together. Reluctantly, I agreed to see her alone.

A nagging sense of apprehension nibbled at the edges of my consciousness as I waited for Bonnie to arrive the next day. I turned it this way and that but couldn't put my finger on what was bothering me. Was I missing something? Was it me, or was I responding to something about her? But when she entered the room the tension in her speech and body language that was evident the week before was so diminished that I relaxed my vigilance.

Since she'd never been in therapy before, she had lots of how, what, when, and why questions. I believe that where it's possible and won't endanger the therapy patients deserve honest answers to their questions. But long experience has also taught me that the only way to understand what happens in the therapeutic process is to do it. After answering several questions, I told her that, but her anxiety rose instantly, and she responded by saying, "I need to understand; I'm that way about everything." Therapeutic translation: I can't tolerate feeling out of control.

I considered giving her a living demonstration of what therapy would be like by commenting as delicately as I knew how on her difficulty in giving up control of our interaction. But I thought about her past, about how vigilant and untrusting it had left her, and decided to let her do it her way for a little while longer.

A first hour tells a therapist a good deal about what to expect, enough sometimes so that she can forecast the trajectory of the therapy. But as I watched our interaction, something told me I wouldn't be able to make any predictions about Bonnie and the work we would do. I knew, of course, that her need for control would be a central issue and that I would have to find the path between allowing her to feel in control while, at the same time, taking charge of the therapy. But as the hour progressed I felt again the same formless misgivings I'd experienced earlier, the same sense that something was going on in the room that I didn't understand. And that "something" was making me distinctly uncomfortable.

In the months that followed we examined her past and her feelings about it in detail, talked about her work, its problems and its gratification, about her nearly nonexistent social life and the reasons for her isolation, about her vigilance and its cost to her. She talked about her connection to me, about how she never had such a relationship before, about how the strength of her feelings surprised her, about how gratified she was to find that she was capable of that kind of attachment.

Although I know that no therapist does the job alone and was delighted with the work Bonnie had done, I also congratulated myself on this breakthrough, convinced that I'd had exactly the right touch to get us this far. I had long since given up any of my own discomfort with her; I'm certain I couldn't have summoned up that early edgy sensibility I had felt in her presence if I had tried.

But two things continued to trouble me: Jerry and her relationship with him never entered into the therapy. When I asked about it she said that things were going well, that her own therapy had enabled her to make changes in the relationship that were good for both of them. A reasonable response that seemed a little magical to me, but I couldn't see any way to push it further.

The second trouble spot that went nowhere no matter how much we talked about it was her impoverished social life. We had been working together for nearly a year when, after much thought, I invited her to join a group I was running, thinking that group therapy could be useful in helping her to become more comfortable in social relations. She was reluctant at first, saying she didn't want anything to dilute our relationship. I'd raise it from time to time, always to the same response, until she unexpectedly announced one day that she was ready to join the group.

Her entry into the group was uneventful. She was quiet and tense during the first few sessions, but no more than most. In our individual sessions she told me she liked everyone in the group, commented astutely on some of the members, and felt herself becoming more comfortable there. It wasn't many weeks before she was a full-fledged participating member, even talking about Jerry once in a while, although nothing that ever revealed anything about the quality of the relationship.

By now we had settled into a familiar and what seemed to me a comfortable therapeutic alliance. Then one day I answered the phone to be greeted by a very angry man who identified himself as Rob Moreland and shouted, "We need to talk about what's going on with you and my wife."

"Your wife?" I repeated, puzzled. "Who are you and what are you talking about?"

"Don't tell me you don't know who I am," he shouted. "I'm Bonnie Paulsen's husband."

Bonnie's husband! I sat openmouthed, unable to speak. I had been seeing Bonnie for about a year and a half by then and the word *husband* had never crossed her lips. Surely this must be some lunatic guy who thought he had some claim on her. When I finally gathered my wits, I told him I'd never heard of him, had no idea what he was talking about, and concluded with, "I'm sorry but I can't speak with you."

His rage escalated. "You damn well better talk to me or I'll have your license."

Trying to calm him down, I said in a manner I hoped was

soothing, "Look, I don't know who you are or what your relationship is to Bonnie. But whatever it is, it would be unethical for me to continue this conversation, so I'm afraid I have to hang up."

Bewildered, I dropped the phone in its cradle and tried to process what had just happened. The man sounded almost crazed with rage and anxiety. Should I call the police? But what if he really were Bonnie's husband? No, it's not possible; no one could fool me like that. Why would anyone want to spend all that time and money in therapy and withhold such a crucial piece of information. Besides, she came into therapy with Jerry. Surely no man would be a party to such a hoax.

I thought about calling Bonnie but told myself to keep calm and wait until her next session two days later. But old feelings arose: the uneasiness I felt when I first met her, the reserve, the sense that she was unknowable. I wandered around the room restlessly, unable to put Rob Moreland's words out of my mind, torn between convincing myself it was impossible and reminding myself that I'd been around long enough to know that nothing is impossible.

A sharp knock on my door jolted me out of my thoughts. I opened it to find Rob Moreland, his face white with anger, his fist raised to bang once again. Before I could close the door to keep him out, he pushed his way into the office, all the while talking to me, telling me that he meant no harm but that he simply *had to talk with me.*

Since he was a lot bigger than I am, I had no choice but to listen while he told me that he and Bonnie had been married for twelve years. They met in college, married two years after their graduation, moved to the San Francisco Bay Area four years later, and now lived together in a house they owned jointly in one of the outlying suburbs. I heard what he said; I had no doubt he was speaking the truth, but it was a while before my mind could really take it in. When I finally found my voice and my wits, I told him once again that it would be unethical for me to say anything, but that if he would come back with Bonnie at seven that evening we could talk then.

"What if she won't come?" he asked.

"She'll come," I assured him with more confidence than I felt. "Just tell her I'm expecting her."

When he left I phoned Bonnie at work and left a message telling her that I wanted to see her at seven. I did the best I could with the four patients I had yet to see that day, but no one got their money's worth.

I waited impatiently as the hands of the clock moved too slowly toward seven. Who was this woman I thought I knew? What could she possibly say to explain the enormity of her lie? What didn't I know yet? The answer, it turned out, was a lot.

When they arrived, Rob was tense but no longer so angry; Bonnie, not surprisingly, was excruciatingly uncomfortable. Even I, who was furious at her betrayal of my trust, couldn't help feeling sorry for her. As soon as we were seated, Rob looked at her levelly and asked the question that had been in my mind all day. "Why?"

Her eyes never left the floor as she shook her head mutely. Finally she lifted her head, stared at us with eyes gone blank, and choked out the words "I don't know."

"That's not good enough," I said. "You did it, you must have some idea what you were after. But before we get into the why question, I need to hear the whole story. So let's start from the beginning."

By now, of course, I had no idea whether anything she had told me was true, nor did I think I could count on Bonnie to tell me. So I literally went back to the beginning and asked Rob what he knew about her family and the circumstances of her birth. He knew the family well, spent many holidays with them over the years, and thought they were good and loving parents. Yes, she was an adopted child; no, she hadn't been abandoned on someone's doorstep. Her parents adopted her at birth and took her home right from the hospital. He always knew Bonnie had some issues about being adopted and that she never felt at home in the family, although he couldn't understand why since they seemed to care for her a lot.

He talked about their lives together, about his job that brought them from east to west, about Bonnie's excitement in the move, about the pleasure they took in exploring this region of the country, so different from their own. But over the years things changed. They became increasingly distant from each other and almost wholly isolated socially. He liked some of the guys at work, and played racquetball with them, but Bonnie never wanted to spend time with them and their wives. She had no friends except for Jerry, a colleague of hers, who had become his friend, too. He sometimes wondered whether there was something more than friendship between Bonnie and Jerry, he said, but he didn't *really* think so. Then, in what seemed to me to be a non sequitur but to him an explanation, "Bonnie has a bad back."

That was news to me, but before I could question it, he continued, saying that she really didn't have time for an affair because for the last two years she spent every week night, from Monday to Friday, in the hospital where she went for traction and some special kind of shots into her spine. The only nights she had off were Saturdays and Sundays, and they were always together on those nights.

Stunned, I turned to Bonnie and asked, "Were you in the

hospital those nights?" knowing before she spoke that she wasn't. As she told it, she came home from work, ate dinner with Rob, then he would drive her to the hospital. He would drop her at the front entrance, she would leave through another door where Jerry was waiting to take her back to the apartment they shared. About once a week, Jerry joined them for dinner. On those nights he'd offer to save Rob the trip, and they could bypass the hospital routine and go straight to their apartment.

If the revelations I'd already heard left me dumbfounded, the depth and breadth of the hoax I was listening to shocked me into near insensibility. I was staggered when I thought about the amount of collusion required of these two men. Jerry was an open participant, but why would he do it? Why would he come to therapy and help her perpetuate the lie? And Rob? We all manage at times not to know what we know when knowing might threaten something we hold dear. But only someone who willfully blinds himself to reality could possibly have swallowed whole such an unbelievable story.

My brain whirled as thoughts ricocheted around, bumping into each other and bouncing off so quickly that I couldn't take them in. I, who don't believe in diagnostic categories, reached for a diagnosis, a word, a set of symptoms, anything to help me make sense of what I was hearing. Not surprisingly, it didn't help. For one thing, none of the diagnoses that leaped to mind fit. Bonnie was neither psychotic nor borderline nor a multiple personality. Sociopathic? Maybe, but so what? It only told me she was one of that peculiar breed who was missing a conscience, a con artist. But I already knew that, and I knew, too, that there was more to her than that single word, with all it stood for, could encompass. Yes, something was missing inside her, but I was virtually certain that I'd also seen something there, some possibility of replacing the missing part. Or maybe I just needed to believe that in order to avoid confronting how thoroughly I'd been snookered.

After more than two hours I called a halt to the session. We all needed time to try to understand what had happened, and I needed to figure out where we could go from here. We agreed to meet at eight o'clock the next morning, and I went home wondering how I could continue to see this woman who had lied so egregiously. Did she even know what the truth was?

Truth, in the sense of *truth as fact*, isn't a prerequisite for doing therapy. There are many "truths" for all of us, and the "facts" of a life are wide open to interpretation since we each internalize experience in our unique way. Even twins brought up side by side with the same parents will likely have different stories to tell about many elements of their shared life. What a therapist looks for, therefore, is *truth in experience*. Is the patient telling the truth about his *experience* of his mother as a withholding woman? Maybe she is, maybe not, or at least not as bad as he says. Time and effective therapy will most likely reveal a more nuanced picture of both mother and the relationship. But at the start, his report of his *experience* is all a therapist has to work with, that and her observations of the kind of transference and countertransference that develops between them.

But Bonnie hadn't unconsciously misunderstood or misinterpreted her experience; she had quite consciously written a whole different narrative and presented it as fact. Why? What meaning did this fictitious persona have for her? Was she such an extraordinary liar, or had I been seduced by my own grandiose conviction of my therapeutic powers? She was good, the best, no doubt about it. But I had to face the painful knowledge that my own ego, what I needed to believe I could do, had gotten in the way of my seeing whatever clues might have been there. At the very least, I could look back and know that I wrote off my own early skepticism much too quickly, caught as I was in an unrecognized countertransference born of the gratification I felt at the "breakthroughs" we were making.

I needed help, so I phoned a trusted colleague and ran the facts of the case by him. He listened closely, agreed that we had much to talk about, but was very doubtful about continued treatment. "She's a sociopath," he concluded, "and you know such people don't respond to treatment."

I knew he was right, and I also knew that no matter the lies Bonnie had concocted about how it actually happened, she clearly *felt* that she had been thrown away by the parents who gave her up for adoption. I couldn't do that to her again.

It would be nice to believe it was pure altruism and my feelings about my therapeutic duty that kept me hanging in. But in truth, I had too much of myself invested in Bonnie and the challenge the case presented. I simply couldn't let it go.

Having made the decision to try to continue our work, I was left with two problems: one long term, the other more immediate. Long term the question was what kind of therapeutic stance to adopt. I had no guidelines, nor was anyone I knew able to offer much help. Clearly, I'd have to make it up as we went along, but at that moment I had no idea what the script would look like.

More immediately, I had a decision to make about the group, which was meeting that evening. I couldn't let Bonnie disappear without explanation, and I didn't think I should do the explaining. I had no idea whether she'd be willing to face their hurt and anger, as well as her own humiliation, and tell them herself. But before I could even put the question to her I had to decide: Was it best for her to continue in the group? Was it right for them to have her there? If my answer to both questions was yes, then my task would be to help them past their sense of betrayal so they could see the benefit in allowing her stay.

Bonnie and Rob were seated silently at opposite ends of the waiting room when I went out to get them. Once in the office, Rob spoke up at once. "I tried all night, but I can't think straight; I need time away to figure things out. I've always wanted to be married to Bonnie, and I think I still do, but I don't know who she is anymore."

I suggested that he might want to talk with someone and offered a referral, which he took, then said, his anger rising to cover the pain that was written in his eyes, "I've got to get out of here. I don't mean you any disrespect, but I can't be in the same room with her right now; I want to kill her." With that, he walked out the door.

Bonnie, pale, miserable, and so tense I thought she might break, sat through this exchange with her eyes glued to the floor. She seemed incapable of speech, and since I couldn't think of anything to say, we sat without words for ten minutes or so. Then it occurred to me; this is what the therapy must be for a while. The *talking cure* would retreat before silence.

I don't know how I got there, and had no idea whether I could manage session after session in total silence, let alone how she would fare. I knew only that if she didn't talk, she couldn't lie, and maybe somewhere in the silence she'd find her way to some kind of truth.

But first there were some things that needed to be said. I asked if she wanted to try to continue in therapy and got a wordless nod in response. I told her that since I didn't know what to believe when she spoke, I had decided we should start out this round in silence. At this she lifted her head, her eyes darting around the room like a trapped animal. I was startled by the intensity of her response, but not surprised at her resistance. Words, after all, were her medium, her way of managing the world and her presentation of self. She stared at me for a moment or two, then finally asked, "For how long?"

"I don't know; this is an experiment and I have no idea how or whether it will work. But I hope that if we can be comfortable in silence for a while, we might find our way to a trusting relationship, one in which you can tell the truth and I can believe you."

She was doubtful, unable to imagine fifty minutes of silence any more than I could. "Do I have a choice?"

"There's always a choice, and there's always something gained, something lost with every choice we make. In this case, if you decide not to enter this experiment with me, I'll end our relationship. If you choose to do it, I don't know how it will come out, but at least you'll be giving us both a chance to find out."

She smiled at that, a thin, wan gesture that had not the slightest hint of joy or pleasure. "I guess that doesn't seem like much of a choice. You know I don't want you to throw me away."

I was struck by her choice of words, the same ones she used when talking about having been given up for adoption, and by the fear that underlay them, the conviction that, once she was known, this must be her fate. In that moment my anger evaporated, replaced by a terrible sense of sadness that I thought must mimic the feelings she lived with all the time. I wanted to reach out to her, to say or do something that would offer her some comfort. But since I didn't know who the real Bonnie was, I had no idea what message such a gesture would send. Would the solace she might find in it allow her to relax into thinking all was forgiven and find new ways to deceive me? It was a preview of one of the major difficulties this therapy would hold for me, my inability to trust myself and my intuitive responses, qualities all therapists rely on as they feel their way through the underbrush of thought and feeling the relationship stirs.

The intensity of my feelings and the conflict they stirred rendered me mute for a moment or two. When I finally found words, I said simply, "I don't want to send you away, Bonnie. So what do you say? Are you game to join me in this gamble?"

She agreed and together we decided that we'd meet four times a week for a while. Now came the other hard part. "There's one more thing we need to resolve. Are you willing to go to the group this evening and tell the truth."

In a voice so small I could hardly hear her, she asked, "Will they talk to me?"

I couldn't give her any reassurance about the group's response since I had no idea what it would be. Although I knew I'd do nothing to seriously compromise the group's cohesion and the working alliance its members had forged, I did tell Bonnie that I'd encourage them to listen to her, would support her remaining in the group, and hoped they would allow her to do so.

That evening I opened the meeting by saying that Bonnie had something to tell them. She spoke hesitantly, her head down, her voice not much above a whisper — the poster girl for contrition. But she told the truth. At first they listened intently, but as they grasped the enormity of her deceit, they became restless, shuffling their feet, shifting around in their chairs until finally they were unable to remain silent. They bombarded her with questions, seeking clarification, demanding answers, struggling to understand. But she couldn't answer the one thing that troubled them most: Why did she do it?

We spent the rest of that session and several more dealing

with their uncomprehending anger and hashing out whether to extrude Bonnie from the group. The seven other members — four men and three women — broke down as I expected. The three who were the most self-protective threatened to quit if she stayed, arguing that they couldn't do therapy with an "untrustworthy liar" in the room. The two who tended to be caretakers thought Bonnie could be saved. The one who was most indecisive was caught in the middle; and the seventh took her usual role as therapist's helper and argued strongly that it was in their interest to work this through with Bonnie in the group. Whatever their divisions about Bonnie's fate, however, they were united in their anger at me — for bringing her into the group, for putting them in the position where they had to waste their precious therapy time dealing with something that most thought wasn't their business, for not knowing she was lying, for, in other words, not being perfect.

I've long believed that one of the dangerous seductions of being a therapist is the kind of authority our patients give over to us and that we too often encourage. So I told myself that it was good for them to come face-to-face with the fact that I wasn't omniscient, that I had no magical insight into another's mind if a person chose to hide it from me, that I could and did make mistakes. But no one likes to be thrust off the pedestal, and I was no different. I reminded myself that it comes with the territory and would pass, but it was small comfort, especially when they were hammering me with the same questions I'd been asking of myself. So I struggled to seal off my defensive response and listened with as much grace as I could muster, which wasn't always as much as I would have wished for.

After all the drama, threats, and arguments, the members agreed to allow Bonnie to stay. Meanwhile, during the month when all this Sturm und Drang was going on in the group, I was meeting with Bonnie in sessions during which we spent fifty minutes in silence, the only communication between us being a nod when she entered and another at the end of the hour. The quiet was so complete I could hear the ticking of the small clock on my desk half a room away. I'm not much good at sitting still for so long without distraction and, as the hours piled up, my internal restlessness increased. And so did my anger — anger at Bonnie for putting us into this position, anger at myself for letting us get there.

I wondered, not for the first time, why I did this work, whether it had any use, whether I knew what I was doing, whether I was good enough, smart enough, perceptive enough to do it right. Then I looked at Bonnie, pale, distraught, yet appearing day after day for what clearly was torture for her, and felt hopeful in the face of her bravery in seeing this through. If she can do it, I told myself, who are you to complain?

After the first few weeks the silence became easier, sometimes almost companionable, and I began to have tea and cookies, which we shared wordlessly. From time to time she'd start to say something, to apologize, to try make it right, but I'd hold my hand up in a gesture that said "wait," and silence her. "Before we can talk, we need to get comfortable enough to trust each other in silence," I'd tell her. "I'm not there yet, and I doubt that you're ready either."

Six weeks later we began to speak, hesitantly at first, then more confidently. With the real story before us, we went back over her life, her night dreams (although they were few) and her daydreams, in an effort to understand what motivated the false one, what purpose it served. Part of the deal I made with her was that when in doubt I could check up on her story by talking to Rob. So from time to time, he and I had a phone conversation about what was going on in their joint lives. She told me that they decided on a formal separation, although neither was willing to tell their parents yet. Rob confirmed that she had moved out and was living with Jerry. From what I had seen of Jerry, I assumed that he would simply repeat whatever Bonnie said, so I saw no point in talking to him. Bonnie, however, told me that, now that their relationship was out in the open, they were planning a life together.

We talked often about finding her birth mother, a quest I encouraged since it seemed to me that knowing the woman who gave her life and why she had had to give her up might help Bonnie feel less like a reject. Several months after our immersion in silence ended, she decided to undertake the search and asked her mother for the name of the agency from which she had been adopted. She carried the information around in her purse for weeks, then one day announced that she had spoken to someone at the agency and would leave the next day to meet with her.

The laws governing anonymity in adoptions were tighter then than they are now, but she got enough information to find the small town her birth mother lived in and some clues as to who her family might be. She traveled there at once, spent hours in the public library tracking down town records, and found the family she thought might be hers. That evening she phoned me, so excited she barely waited for my hello before she shouted into the phone, "Lillian, you won't believe it. I think I found my mother and she has brown eyes just like mine. I actually look like someone."

She came back the next day, worrying over when and how to make contact, asking herself whether she really wanted to do it. Several days later she called me crying, the first tears she shed in all the time I'd known her. She had telephoned the woman she thought was her mother and identified herself with her birth date and the date of her adoption. She heard a short, sharp intake of breath, then without a word, the woman hung up. She tried calling back every few minutes for over an hour but the phone was obviously off the hook. "What do I do now?" she wept.

I assumed her birth mother needed time to get used to the idea that she'd been found and suggested that Bonnie wait until Sunday when people in a small town are typically back from church and eating their afternoon meal. It seemed a long way to Sunday, but she agreed to wait and asked me to be with her when she made the call. She arrived at my office a little early and waited nervously for the appointed hour. When she finally dialed the number, a man answered and, even before she finished introducing herself, he asked, his tone hesitant as if he already knew the answer, "Who are you?"

Bonnie repeated the information she'd given the woman a few days earlier while I stood beside her, my throat tight, my heart constricted. We heard a gasp, then "Oh my God," then silence. But the line remained open. We waited, nearly breathless with anxiety.

After what seemed like an interminable time, he collected himself enough to ask some questions. Bonnie told him what she knew about her birth and adoption. He listened quietly as he absorbed the facts she put before him, then said, "Thank God; we've waited a long time. Where are you calling from?"

"Berkeley," she replied.

"You mean Berkeley in California?"

When she assured him that was indeed what she meant, this man who had given her up for adoption thirty-five years earlier shouted, "What, a daughter of mine lives in that Sodom and Gomorrah? You can't stay there. I'll send you a ticket tomorrow so you can come home right now."

It was the one light moment of the conversation, the one Bonnie and I would laugh about for a long time after.

She assured him that Berkeley wasn't as bad as its press notices and gave him the bare facts of what she labeled her "very
ordinary life." She had lots of questions for him, but she
couldn't yet speak the one that haunted her: Why did you give
me away?

During the next half hour they exchanged stories. When
she could contain it no longer, she asked about her birth. He
told her that he and his wife had known each other all their
lives, that they knew from the time they were in high school
they'd marry one day, that they'd gone to college together and
gotten pregnant during their junior year.

"Why did you give me away if you and my mother knew
you were going to get married anyway?" she finally asked in a
voice so tight with emotion that it barely escaped her throat.

It was a different time, he explained, his words calm but his
tone pleading for understanding. They lived in a very small
town where everyone knew them, and women just didn't have
babies "out of wedlock." They couldn't face the shame of what
he called a "shotgun wedding"; their families would never have
forgiven them. "We didn't think we had a choice. But," he assured her, "much as we love our sons, your brothers, they
never made up for the loss we felt about having to give you up."

Finally, reluctantly, they said good-bye with the promise
that they would talk the next day to arrange a meeting.

During the conversation Bonnie had seemed completely
open and responsive. But when she hung up she was quiet and
thoughtful, as if she didn't know what to make of the ease with
which it had all happened. She was glad it was over, she said,
but she hadn't expected this kind of greeting and it made her
uncomfortable. "I don't even know them, and he's talking like
he's my father and can tell me where to live."

She knew she'd have to meet them but was ambivalent
about when and how she wanted it to happen. And she defi-

nitely wasn't prepared to go there and take on the whole family. So for the next few days, during which she dealt with her ambivalence and anxieties, she managed to avoid her birth father's phone calls. Finally, she decided that she'd ask them to come to visit her, and they agreed on a meeting the following week. She called me feeling anxious, wondering if she was doing the right thing, uncertain whether she wanted to know them, and asking if she could come in with them. I, of course, was bursting with curiosity and wouldn't have missed it.

A week later the three of them came into my office, her father complaining that he'd never met a "headshrinker" before and wondering why his daughter needed one. "I thought you people only lived on TV," he said, softening his comment with a winning smile. Most stunning was the resemblance between Bonnie and her birth mother. She didn't just look like someone, she was a carbon copy of her mother, right down to the shape of her ears.

I spent the next two hours listening to them exchanging stories about their lives. Her birth parents wanted reassurance that they hadn't injured her, that she had been brought up by good people who loved her. Bonnie gave it, although that wasn't the story she usually told. I knew it was all too good to be true, that the day of reckoning would come and they'd have to work through the issues that would surely lie between them, not least Bonnie's anger about being given away. But this wasn't the time for that, and I stayed out of their way and watched with pleasure as they got acquainted.

After a while Bonnie and her newfound family settled into a routine of weekly phone calls and occasional visits. She and I continued to meet twice a week and once again the therapy seemed to be progressing well. On the outside, she reported satisfaction with her professional life where she moved to a new job that promised a bright future. On the emotional level, she evidenced a new self-awareness, greater connection to her feelings, and more insight into her behavior, past and present. Her relationship with Jerry, she said, was "better than it had ever been."

I was too wary to return to my former self-congratulatory state, but I couldn't help feeling pleased with her progress in both our individual work and the way she functioned in the group. She didn't form any friendships there as others did, but she participated well in the sessions and developed a comfortable rapport with two of the members, a man and a woman.

The months piled up into three years, during which time Bonnie never missed a session, not even when she was sick. Then one Monday, about an hour before she was due to come in, she phoned and left word saying her car had broken down and she would see me at her next scheduled hour, which was on Thursday. I was mildly surprised, since her car had a habit of breaking down and, always before, she managed to get to my office. But the following days were busy, and I gave it no more than a passing thought. Until she didn't show up for her session on Thursday.

That evening I phoned and got a recording that said the telephone had been disconnected and there was no forwarding number. I called Rob who was as puzzled as I was. They had talked earlier in the week about some financial matters and she had said nothing about moving. The next day I phoned her office and was told that she had a family emergency and had to take an unexpected leave. I left a message for Jerry and wondered if he'd call back. An hour later he did. He had no idea where Bonnie had gone. He had been away at a family event over the weekend that she hadn't wanted to attend and when he came back on Sunday night, her clothes were gone. Since they each had their own phone numbers, he didn't know until I told him that hers had been disconnected.

I never saw Bonnie again.

In the years since then I've found myself thinking about her from time to time, wondering who she really is, whether it's possible for anyone, including her, to know, and not least, what else I might have done to resolve these now unanswerable questions. I suppose there's a lesson to be learned in this story, but I'm still not sure what it is except the one I've always known: Any patient who puts her mind to it can defeat even the most artful and accomplished therapist. The problem, as I have been known to tell patients who have tried my soul, is "When you win, you lose."

Except in this case Bonnie did win one thing. She may have disappeared from my life, but I'll never be able to throw her out of my mind. She lives there, engraved in my brain, a puzzle with no solution.

To Live or Die

Jake Garvin was part of Berkeley's academic left, a group that, despite the university's worldwide reputation for political radicalism, was small enough so that most lefties either knew or knew about each other. Since I received my doctoral degree from Berkeley, did part of my postdoctoral clinical training there, and had been active in student, anti–Vietnam War, and feminist politics during the period when those movements arose, I was known in the left as a therapist who could be trusted. By which they meant someone who wouldn't dismiss their political concerns and activities as displaced adolescent rebellion against authority, as so much psychological analysis did then. And unfortunately, still does. Not, mind you, that I didn't think that was true for some of the student activists of the time. But whatever their individual psychological issues may have been, they also had legitimate social and political grievances that needed redress.

Jake was a member of a brash group of Young Turks in the social sciences and humanities, all of them advanced graduate students or newly appointed assistant professors on the first rung of a long tenure ladder, all challenging the established theoretical and methodological assumptions of their disciplines, all seeking to move the university out of its ivory tower and into the streets. I knew some of them, thought they had interesting (if sometimes overstated) things to say, and appreciated the fact that they were making waves that rocked their various disciplinary boats. Although I didn't know Jake personally, I'd seen him around enough to wonder about the manic energy he gave off.

I had been in practice just a few years when he called for an appointment. Like most beginning therapists, I was still surprised when anyone called for my services, a feeling that was heightened substantially when I realized who was at the other end of the line. I never figured him for a therapy candidate. His public image was too cocky, too challenging of existing authority, too anti-establishment.

He spoke rapidly, the words seeming to tumble over one another with the same manic edge I'd noticed in public. In a tone that sounded more like a command than a request, he announced that he had only two hours when he was available to see me. The therapist in me understood that his manner was a defensive maneuver, probably born of his discomfort in having to ask for help. Still, I found myself irritated with his peremptory style and barely restrained myself from a sarcastic reminder that I, too, had a life.

In fact, I had no free clinical hour in the following week. I told myself that I could free up an hour from time set aside for writing, which I did occasionally when faced with what seemed like a clinical emergency. But I was torn between not wanting to accommodate his arrogance and curiosity about why he wanted to see a therapist. Curiosity won.

I offered him an hour, not one of the two he asked for, which were taken by patients who came each week at those times. He was nonplussed, as if it never occurred to him I might be busy, then finally said edgily, "Look, my schedule's very tight and those are the only hours I can spare for this." Not a response to endear him to my therapist's heart.

It was getting harder to keep my cool, to refrain from a remark that wondered why, if this was such a low priority, he was bothering to call. But I managed to hold my tongue and said simply, "I'm sorry, those hours are taken and won't be available for some time."

I could almost hear his struggle to contain his anger as he

took in my refusal. "Can't you change one of them to some other time?"

By then I was sorry I had allowed curiosity to reign and said, not very kindly, "I'm afraid they have schedules, too, but I'd be happy to refer you to someone else who might be able to accommodate your needs."

"No, I want to see you; I just wish you weren't so damn uncooperative."

I laughed. "It sounds as if it comes as a surprise to you that I have a life and a work schedule, and that I wasn't sitting around waiting for you to call."

At that he seemed to back up, take a look at himself and the interaction he had set in motion, and said, "Sorry, I guess I came on pretty strong, huh. I do that sometimes."

One for him, I thought, my irritation falling away like an unwelcome cloak. We were both quiet for a moment while I took in the quick shifts in my feelings, trying to figure out what this meant for the work we'd do together, and wondering which way he'd go. Finally, he spoke. "Okay, I'll take that time if it's really all you've got."

Our business finished, I started to say good-bye when he interrupted. "Is it?"

Not sure what he wanted, I asked.

"Is it really all you've got?"

"Yes, it is. But I'm wondering why you ask. Did you think I was playing some kind of a game with you?"

"It's what shrinks do, isn't it?" he replied, sounding angry again.

"Not this one," I said, then closed the conversation with the reminder of the hour we'd agreed upon and hung up.

I was taking advantage of a canceled session and was at my computer, writing, when the bell announced Jake's arrival a week later. I glanced at the clock: ten minutes early. I wouldn't expect him to be early, I thought, not after the fuss he made about his busy schedule. But right then I was more concerned with trying to put a messy sentence in order, so I continued my labors. Two minutes later the bell rang again, this time followed quickly by a loud knock on the door.

Irritated once again by his imperious behavior, I left my desk and went to the door. I opened it to find him restlessly pacing the length of the waiting room, so engaged in whatever was going on in his head that he didn't see me in the doorway. I watched him quietly, somewhat taken aback by what I saw. On campus, where he was an outspoken leader, he seemed larger, more substantial than the relatively small, wiry, almost delicate-boned man I was observing. Where in public he exuded confidence and certainty, here there was only tension and anxiety. A startling difference that left me thinking about how much our perceptions of another are colored by context. In a setting where he was in charge, he seemed larger than life; in my office, where he was just another anxious patient, he looked smaller. Neither, obviously, the sum of the man.

He stopped in his tracks when he noticed me, his expression registering a flicker of surprise as if he were trying to process who I was and why he was there. With a visible effort he pulled himself into the present, then with a small crooked smile to soften the words "It's about time."

I knew he was expecting a response in kind, but I smiled and stepped aside, inviting him in wordlessly. He entered the room warily, his watchful dark eyes sweeping every corner, and ignored my gesture pointing him to the chair usually reserved for patients. Instead, he seated himself at the far end of the room so that I had to swivel my chair around to face him.

We were silent for a moment, watchful, each of us waiting and wondering what would come next. Even seated he seemed in motion, every line of his body revealing a man who lived intensely and at high speed. A scar swept down the left side of his long, narrow face, and disappeared into a full mustache that complimented the ponytail that was the order of the day for those who had visions of a new social order.

I wondered, as I watched him, what he was seeing. Did I look as different to him in this new setting as he did to me? As if he read my mind, he remarked, "You look different."

"Can you say how I seem different?"

"I don't know exactly, you just look bigger, I guess. When I see you around, you look small, you know, like you're a little person."

Just the opposite of my disparate images of him. Should I tell him that? Before the thought fully cohered, all the supervisors I ever had jumped on my shoulder and shouted no. Why not? I asked silently, unable to make up my mind whether it was a real question or an argument. But I didn't have to think very long before I decided they were right. Maybe it would be useful to share my initial inverted impressions somewhere down the line, but right now it was important for both of us to understand his reaction to me. "So what do you make of that?" I asked.

"I don't know; maybe I never really looked at you before," he replied, not really believing his own words.

"You don't sound convinced."

"Yeah, well, it's sort of strange, don't you think? It really seems like you're a lot bigger, like you're two different people."

"Maybe you need to see me as bigger than you thought because you've come to me for help."

"And what?" he asked crossly. "I'm reassured by my big mama? Maybe you can cut the shrink shit and let me tell you why I'm here."

I know we therapists tell our patients that they can say anything that comes to mind. But I've never understood why they take that to mean that flat-out rudeness, or worse yet, personal insults, are acceptable. A few years ago I was seeing a woman I'll call Sandra, who spent the better part of several sessions hurling insults at me while refusing to hear anything I said in response. I tried every trick I knew, but nothing stopped her until one day I said quietly, but in a voice so firm it brooked no argument, "Enough! You may not talk to me like that anymore."

The torrent of words skidded to a halt while she stared at me uncomprehending. Finally, her mind back in gear, she said with genuine surprise, "But I thought that's what I'm supposed to do here, say whatever I'm thinking."

"Yes," I replied, "but that doesn't mean you can vilify me for weeks just because you feel like it and refuse to examine what you're doing and why. The task here is not only to say what you think, but to think about what you say."

She looked at me chastened and said, as much to herself as to me, "But my last therapist never stopped me."

"Maybe that's why you're still in therapy," I replied testily.

Sometimes, as with Sandra, such behavior is a test, much like a small child who pushes at the boundaries of the acceptable. But with Jake it was all part of the ornery persona he had presented from our first phone conversation, which itself was born of his attempt to feel less vulnerable by stripping me of whatever power and authority went with my role.

Unfortunately, understanding someone's behavior doesn't always make it go down any more easily, so the contained therapist in me had to fight off the impulse of my wounded ego to strike back. One side was so annoyed with Jake's "shrink shit" comment that I toyed with a confrontation that interpreted his behavior as part of his power struggle with me, while the other side reminded me that we'd both lose if I picked up the gauntlet. In the end, I shrugged off his comment, said "Okay," and made a gesture indicating that the floor was his.

He leaned forward, his elbows resting on his knees, chin on his fists, and searched for a way to start. Finally, hesitantly, he began, "I read a couple of your books; they're good, especially the one about working-class families. A lot of it was like reading about my own life. And since I'm having trouble writing my dissertation, I thought you could help me. I've got all the data I need, had it for the last couple of years, maybe more. I just can't get it written."

Interesting, I thought. He started by talking about how my book on working-class family life touched his own experience and ended up sounding as if he were asking me for writing lessons. Again, I was tempted to share my observation, partly to show off my smarts and cut through his cocksure posturing. But this time I knew without much struggle that it wasn't the time and asked him instead to tell me about his project.

We talked about it for a while, an interesting conversation that reflected a keen intelligence and deep knowledge of his subject. It's easy for me to get caught up in this kind of discussion of ideas, and early in my clinical career I worried about it, especially since many of my patients were university-based men who often retreated behind ideas as a way of avoiding their personal and interpersonal issues. So I fretted about how to deal with Jake: Am I colluding with his avoidance if I continue this intellectualized conversation? Or is this the only way to build a relationship from which we can get to the next step?

Now, all these years later, I know the answer. Doing therapy isn't some set of prescribed acts based on preexisting rules; it's a process that differs from patient to patient and therapist to therapist. It's why it's so hard to teach. As an experienced and successful colleague remarked to me recently, "I know what works for me, but I can't really teach it to anyone else because we all have to find our own voice and our own way of approaching each relationship."

With Jake, the important thing was to gain his trust and respect, which even then I knew intuitively would come first through his head, not his heart. So we talked about his work. By the end of that first session I had him interested, not in me as a therapist but as a colleague who could share ideas about his work. It wasn't all I wanted, but it was a start. As we were setting up our next appointment, he asked hesitantly, "I was wondering, how would it be if I brought you something to read?"

I knew the dangers of saying yes. It's hard enough to read and respond critically to a colleague's work without injured feelings and misunderstandings. How would we manage it as patient and therapist, especially when we didn't yet have a solid relationship? To say yes would violate all I had been taught about maintaining tight control of the boundaries between us. But I couldn't just say no. It was clearly hard for him to ask; to be refused would feel like a humiliation. So I hedged and said, "I'm interested in your work and would be pleased to read it, but first we have to talk about how to manage it, given that we have this complicated relationship where we're both colleagues and therapist and patient. So let's do that next time, when we have time to decide together whether it's a good idea."

When he came back the following week, he was even speedier than he had been earlier, his speech so fast and stressed that I had to strain hard to follow what he was saying. Despite his obvious tension, however, his manner was friendly as he raised again the question of my reading his work, said he'd heard from students of mine that I was a tough critic, and assured me that he was able to accept "anything you throw at me."

I said I knew he wanted to believe that his problem with the work was intellectual, but I saw it as an emotional issue, something out of consciousness that was disabling him. If I agreed to read his work, I was afraid it would interfere with the emotional work he had to do. But even as I spoke, I knew he didn't "get it," that for him the work created the emotional problem, not the other way around. So rather than continue to talk about it, I said, "Why don't we see how this hour goes, how much we can get into the work I think you need to do?"

"Okay, how do we do that?"

"Well, you start by telling me something about yourself."

"Like what? Like I'm thirty-two years old and still a student? Like I got married and divorced in less than a year because I was a disaster as a husband? Believe me, that's a very short story."

He couldn't or wouldn't say much more about what happened in his marriage, insisting that it was in the past and of no importance. Responding to my question about whether there was a woman in his life, he said that he didn't "need that complication right now," that his first priority was getting his degree and getting out of Berkeley. He had two job offers, both dependent on his finishing his dissertation in the next year, which was why it was urgent that we "stop fooling around with this other stuff and deal with the problem at hand."

Still looking for a way into the "other stuff," I said, "Okay, let's talk about your writing. I know you've written at least one article during these years when you say you haven't been able to write. Do you have any idea why you could do that and can't do the dissertation?"

He looked at me inquiringly but didn't reply.

"I'm trying to understand if there's something significant about the time frame," I explained. "Has anything else happened in the years since you finished collecting your data that might make writing it up difficult?"

He shrugged, his face a blank, and began to talk about the project.

I listened halfheartedly, feeling frustrated and trying to keep my impatience in check. Finally, I knew I had to speak, even if it meant losing him. "After listening to you for the last half hour, it's clear to me that, whatever is getting in your way, it's not a lack of thinking or writing skills. I don't know what the problem is, but one thing I do know: You're not going to get very far up the mountain you're trying to climb by approaching it head-on like this. In my experience, these are the times when you get further by going around an obstacle rather than trying to bulldoze your way through it."

"You mean by telling you about my tragic childhood," he replied with a nasty sneer.

"I mean by letting me know who you are and how you got that way. You can discount what I say with that dismissive sneer, you can decide not to come back, or you can come back and behave in ways that will defeat the work we have to do. But beware. This is one of those moments in life when if you win, you lose."

"What the hell does that mean?"

"Just what I said. I don't want to spar with you, Jake. I think we can work effectively together if you'll let us. But that means I need to know something about your past, tragic or not, as well as what's going on in your personal and emotional life in the present. Why, for example, do you seem to be wound so tightly?"

He sat there staring at me, trying to make up his mind whether to leave or accede to my demand. Finally, with a sigh, "Okay, you win. What do you want to know?"

Even when he was giving in, he had a way of saying things that touched my own smart-ass tendency, and I had to keep myself from retorting, "No, you win if you do it my way." Instead, I said, "Let's start by talking about your family and what it was like growing up there."

He was quiet for a few minutes, his eyes flitting nervously around the room as if looking for an escape, not just from the task ahead but from the emotions roiling inside him. When he finally found words, all he could say for a while was "I don't even know where to start, it was such a mess."

Then his eyes on the floor, he began to speak. His father and mother met in Germany when his father was part of the United States occupation army in the aftermath of World War II. "It wasn't," he said caustically, "a marriage made in heaven. I guess it was every German girl's dream to marry an American and come here to live the good life, but that sure as hell isn't what my mother got. My father was a sick, angry guy who never held a job for long because he couldn't get along with anybody. Bad as it was when he was working, it got worse when he wasn't because then he was drunk most of the time. I mean he drank a lot all the time, but all bets were off when he quit or got canned. He was hospitalized the first time when I was thirteen with what you people call *manic-depressive psychosis*. After that he was in and out a half dozen times before he finally died a couple of years ago."

I listened quietly to this all-too-familiar tale of a father's episodic unemployment that became increasingly frequent, and the alcoholic rages that grew in duration and intensity with each failure. I winced inside as I heard yet another story of a mother's stoic passivity as she tended her son's wounds and tried to explain his father's behavior away. But I was struck most immediately by the fact that his father's death coincided with the same time period when he found himself unable to write. "Does it strike you that your father died about the same time you began to have trouble with your work?"

"There you go with that shrink shit again. It doesn't *strike me* at all," he said, his tone mimicking mine. "If you really want to know, I didn't give a damn whether he lived or died. And don't tell me I should feel sorry for him because he was nuts. Forget it! I don't want to hear any of that forgiveness crap. I've heard it before from other shrinks, and I'm out of here if I have to listen to it again. Sick or not, he was one lousy, fucking bastard, and I don't owe him a damn thing. See this scar," he said, pointing to the gash on his face, his voice tight with rage, "he gave me this. It's why he ended up in the hospital that first time. My mother finally stood up to him, first time, and called the cops, but only because she was afraid he'd kill me."

Hearing Jake's bitter denunciation of his parents and his unforgiving posture brought to the fore my own thoughts and feelings about the hold the idea of forgiveness has on our collective imagination, about how politically incorrect it is in our society to be unwilling to forgive, about how harsh the word *unforgiving* sounds, even to my ears. I, who have written about the tyranny of the belief, preached so insistently by our twin gods, religion and psychology, that only in forgiveness will we find healing. In fact, some things are unforgivable, high among them parents who seriously abuse the children they're supposed to love and protect. Moreover, the promise that forgiveness will ease our pain is not only questionable but can be psychically dangerous, since it too often leads us into legislating away authentic, if unpleasant, feelings in search of those we're told we *ought* to have.

It's that conflict, the conflict between our denied feelings and the attempt to dictate "appropriate" ones, that's often at the heart of the neurotic problems therapists see. I don't dismiss the possibility of forgiveness, nor do I think it is without value. But years of watching people try to make themselves feel what they believe they *should* feel (Of course I love my mother; she didn't mean to hurt me. No, I never wanted to hurt my little sister; it's not her fault she was so pretty. My father didn't mean to be cruel, he was sick.) has convinced me that in our struggle with the hurts of the past, we need to look not for forgiveness but for understanding — understanding of ourselves, understanding of the other. Only then can we put away the angry bitterness that can corrode the soul. If forgiveness comes out of the process, it will be an authentic experience, one that grows from inside, not one imposed from without. But it's not the only path to resolution, and sometimes not even the best one.

Jake spoke in anger, but it was his pain just below the surface that caught my attention. Pain, and something like fear. It's not unusual in families with serious mental illness for a child to live with dread that the "curse" will follow him. And the manic-depressive syndrome, as it was called then (now renamed *Bipolar II*), is known to be heritable. With Jake's own manic style, it was something to fear. Was this what he was trying so hard to escape with the frenetic pace of his life?

I was relieved to notice our time was up. I needed time to think about how to use the material I now had, where I could push Jake and where it was best to leave his defenses alone. I still didn't know whether it was a good or bad idea to read his work, and I knew what most of my colleagues would say if I asked their advice. But it seemed clear that he chose me and not another therapist because he knew I could relate to his intellectual work since it wasn't far off from my own, and that this was the way I could cement a connection between us. So, despite my reservations, I said as he was leaving, "Bring what you'd like me to read next week."

He looked surprised, gave me a rare smile, and said simply, "Thanks."

He came to our next session bearing a manila envelope,

which he dropped on my desk. "I'll read it before our next meeting," I said, "but right now I think we should talk about your father and your relationship with him."

"Uh-oh. Back to being a shrink again, huh. Look, I don't mean to give you a hard time, but I've done that already, more than once, and it never took. I don't know if I want to do it again."

"Then why are you in a therapist's office?"

He smiled and made an attempt at a joke, "Because I knew you'd be good for my work."

"If that's all you wanted, you could have gotten that free just by asking for a meeting to discuss your project, as I'm sure you do with colleagues all the time. Look, I understand your skepticism, and maybe it's even well founded. But since we're both here and you clearly intend to keep coming, let's make a deal. You give me what I want, which is some access to your internal life, and I'll give you what you want, which is to read and respond to your work."

"Boy, I've got to hand it to you," he said with grudging admiration, "you're some persistent shrink. But you've got to believe me when I say I don't know what else to say about him except that he was a son of a bitch, and I hated him. I was seventeen when I left home with a college scholarship, and I never looked back. I went home a couple of times to see my mom, but she died my junior year, and that was it. She wasn't even that sick when she died. I always figured she just gave it up because she didn't want to live with him anymore and couldn't figure another way out."

His remark sent me back into my own childhood, to memories of my father's death when I was five years old from an illness that rarely kills anyone, to my conviction from the time I was old enough to have such thoughts that he allowed himself to get sick enough to die because it was the only way he could get away from my mother, to my own fantasies about suicide when life with her felt unbearable. I shook the thoughts away and wrenched myself back to Jake's story with a heightened sense of compassion and identity with him.

"I didn't see my father for years after that until he looked me up a few months before he died. He was already sick, lung cancer, and knew he was going to die, so I guess he wanted to make peace. Like I could suddenly forget how he fucked me over and say, "'Hey, Dad, glad you're here; all is forgiven.' No way."

"Yet your writing problems started, or at the very least got substantially worse, at about the same time he died. It's hard to believe that's just a coincidence."

He didn't answer. Puzzled, I pushed harder. "What is it, Jake? Why won't you talk about this?" Then a shot in the dark, "Did he 'fuck you over' by bequeathing his manic-depressive illness to you? Is that what you're so frightened of?"

He jumped out of the chair and nearly lunged across the room. "Dammit, I'm not crazy; I'm not," he shouted as he stood over me, his eyes blazing with some combination of hatred and anguish. "Okay, is this what you wanted to know? Yeah, that's what that fucking bastard left me; that's my inheritance; I'm a manic-depressive just like him."

With that he sank to the floor at my feet and wept. I waited for him to quiet a bit, then moved out of my chair and sat next to him. "You may have his illness, but that doesn't mean you're like him."

"How will I ever know that?" he asked, not really a question but a statement of his hopelessness.

"Your life will tell you when you live it differently."

"How do I do that? I won't take those damn pills anymore," he insisted, referring to Lithium, which was at the time the only effective medication for manic-depression. "They did keep my mind from racing so fast, and the noise in there got quieter, but I felt like a zombie." A common complaint from patients who take Lithium, and the reason so many refuse to continue to do so.

It's undoubtedly true that the medication slows a person down, but it's also true that manic-depressives often become so attached to their mania that they can't tolerate losing it. We can't know what it feels like without having lived it, of course, but as I've watched such patients over the years, I've come to understand some of the appeal of the mania — the sense of invulnerability it can bring, the belief that it's the source of creativity, the excitement that comes with the feeling of heightened powers, that anything is possible. For someone coming down from that kind of high, whether through chemistry or the natural rhythm of the disease, the return to something approaching normal functioning can feel unbearably slowed down.

As we came to the end of the session, Jake lingered. He walked to the door, restless, turned back, then back again. Finally, facing the door and away from me, he asked in a voice so low I could hardly hear him, "Do you have any more time this week?"

I responded at once, offering him time on one of my precious writing days. "I'll be here," he mumbled, and hurried out, as if fearful he might change his mind if he tarried.

That evening, curious to see what he'd written, I picked up the envelope Jake left earlier in the day. In it I found the beginnings of two chapters that read like the product of a disordered mind. Here and there I caught a glimpse of some very good ideas, but the chaos on the page made it nearly impossible to make sense of most of it. It was in this written work, far more than in talking to him, that I could see most fully the ruminative, circular, obsessional style that characterized his thought processes. I worried at first that I'd made a mistake, that I shouldn't have been so quick to bypass the rule about not confounding the therapy with anything outside the clinical setting. But I also knew that I'd had a look inside his mind that I wouldn't otherwise have had. So I reassured myself that we'd passed through an important moment together, one that I believed (hoped?) would hold the relationship in place, even in the face of whatever I might say about his work.

Although I was critical of the form when we met next, my enthusiasm for the content of Jake's project, the ideas of his emerging analysis, buoyed him enough so that he began to move out of the stuck place he'd been in for so long. For the next several months Jake came for two sessions a week during which we talked about his work while also probing his internal life. I don't know why I was surprised to see how easily it all flowed together, since I knew from my own experience how many connections there are between the intellectual and emotional. How could it be otherwise for a person whose work is one of the defining features of identity? It's why I agreed to read Jake's work despite the reproachful looks from those who sat on my shoulders.

But what if I had been starting out at twenty-five instead of forty-five, a young person, inexperienced in living as most beginning therapists are? If it was so hard for me to keep wrestling with "them" in those early years, how much more difficult is it for someone who hasn't been tempered by time and experience. How many therapies fail because the therapist has been so thoroughly indoctrinated by the rules that he doesn't dare break them, even when common sense tells him it would be helpful?

As our relationship intensified and Jake became more trusting and more attached, he was looser in talking about his dreams, his fantasies, and his fears, and the noise in his head quieted down substantially. He still didn't write easily, but what he got down on paper was both coherent and smart.

Then one day he arrived with some good but troubling news. He had been awarded a prestigious year-long fellowship in which his only responsibility would be to write his dissertation. But it would take him to the other side of the country. If he stayed in Berkeley, we could continue our work, but he would have all the distractions of being here — his job as a teaching assistant, the political meetings and the work that went with them, the many friends and acquaintances who had some claim on his time and attention. If he took the fellowship, he'd live in a cosseted setting that provided housing, office space, a support staff, and three meals a day.

It looked like a no-brainer. How could he turn down such an extraordinary opportunity? But he was conflicted. He didn't want to go, and he couldn't imagine staying. He had about six weeks to make the decision, and we talked of nothing else. We were both caught. I was the first therapist Jake had ever connected with; he was clearly moving ahead, but it was too soon to break the connection, his progress too fragile. How could I counsel him to go?

But I didn't know how I could counsel him to stay either. I was myself only a few years away from having completed my own dissertation, from the thrill of getting my degree and seeing the doors it opened for me. I knew firsthand what an important turning point it was in my life, in any life. Moreover, anyone who lives around a university knows many people who are what we call ABD (all but the dissertation), men and women who somehow never could finish the job. I knew this was Jake's fear, and it was mine for him. He'd never live easily if he didn't get his degree, and this might be his big chance.

A more important fuel for my doubts was the fact that, even though I was doing therapy, I retained a certain skepticism about the enterprise and what it could accomplish, especially in disorders as serious as manic-depression. Just as I thought that the bargain many psychoanalysts wrested from their patients in those years — the promise that they would make no significant changes in their lives during the course of treatment — was an arrogant conceit.

Certainly, psychotherapy can be helpful in treating many of the emotional ills our patients suffer. But the notion that it's a "cure" for the psychic pain we accumulate in the course of living, or that it can change basic qualities of character, those constitutional givens with which we come into the world and that give form to how we experience and live in it, is a fantasy. So I had no illusions that another year of work (or maybe even ten more years) would make Jake's manic-depressive illness disappear or change his characteristic way of being in the world. And I certainly couldn't offer either one of us any assurance that this year of therapy would be any better for him than taking the fellowship, especially if he didn't finish the dissertation and lost the jobs that were waiting for him.

I ran the facts of the case by several colleagues, whose answers didn't vary much. They all sympathized with Jake's dilemma but all agreed that it was his decision to make, not mine. My job, they said, was only to help him understand the issues underlying his conflict. I left each conversation wondering: What are we expert at if we can't help our patients make the important life decisions that face them?

I thought about a young therapist (I'll call her Nancy) who came into training at the clinic where I was working a few years earlier. It was common knowledge in the therapeutic community that the place had been in turmoil for over a year and wasn't a satisfactory training site. Yet when Nancy was deciding between this and a more suitable place for her internship, her therapist never entered the decision-making process, not even to tell her what she knew. Months later when Nancy was stuck in a setting in which she was miserable, she challenged her therapist, wondering why she hadn't at least warned her about what she was walking into. Unfazed, her therapist replied that it wasn't for her to tell a patient what choices to make and, in any case, there was something for Nancy to learn from her mistakes. Moreover, she said, since it was Nancy's mistake, she should be talking about why she made it, not remonstrating with her therapist. From where I sat, Nancy's "mistake" was that she remained in therapy with that woman.

My problem with Jake, though, was that there was no right or wrong. My heart told me that he should stay and continue our work. He himself acknowledged that he'd found a sense of safety with me that he'd never known before, that hard as the work was sometimes, my office was the one place where he came close to finding some internal peace. But with everyone around me warning against coming down on either side, I couldn't find the inner conviction to speak what I felt. So I did what I was trained to do and helped him weigh the options. I never spoke from my heart, never told him I wanted him to stay, never pushed one side over the other.

The day before the deadline for the decision, he announced that he was taking the fellowship and would be leaving Berkeley in late summer, two months hence. We continued our work, but something had gone out of it. I tried to talk to him about it, about the depression that I feared was closing down on him, but we didn't get very far. I worried that he might feel that I'd abandoned him when I didn't fight for him to stay, and asked him if there was some truth to my concerns. He assured me there was not, said this was the only "reasonable and sensible choice," and nothing I might say would change that. I didn't fully believe him and pushed him hard over the next few sessions, but he held to the same line. A few days before his scheduled departure, I finally asked, "If I were to ask you to stay, would you?"

He searched my face for a while, then said, "But you won't, will you?"

"I will if you want me to."

He walked across the room, leaned down and kissed my cheek, and said, "I wouldn't do that to you."

Jake left Berkeley two days later. We agreed that he'd phone when he got settled and that we'd arrange to speak on the phone each week. I had no idea where to reach him, so had no choice but to wait. Ten worrisome days later, he called, deep into an agitated depression. His mind, he said, wasn't "racing anymore, it's totally stalled, like it's empty except for the noise that won't go away. I can't think," he said, despairing. "I can't do it; I can't."

At the end of an hour's conversation, I finally said what I should have said weeks earlier. "This is too hard, Jake; you don't have to do it. Come home; we'll do it together, I promise."

"I can't," he said. "I *have* to do this here; it's why I came. I can't depend on you; I have to know I can do it. Otherwise, what the hell's any of it worth?"

His tone frightened me. I hadn't thought of him as suicidal when he was here, but now I wondered. I told myself that his eagerness to continue our conversations by phone was reassuring, but a doubt had crept in and wouldn't leave me alone.

We spoke every day for the next two weeks and although he was clearly depressed, he was beginning to work and seemed more hopeful. Then just as I relaxed my vigilance a bit, I picked up my phone one morning to hear a woman's voice say, "This is Elizabeth Garvin, Jake's sister. Jake killed himself last night. He left a note asking me to call you. It says 'Tell Lillian she's the only reason I didn't do it sooner.'"

It's more than a quarter of a century since that phone call, but it still haunts me. Friends and colleagues I spoke with in the aftermath of Jake's suicide all told me I was grandiose to think I could have kept him alive. It's undoubtedly true that I have a somewhat grandiose sense of my efficacy as a therapist; I think it's part of what allows me to take the kind of risks that make me good at what I do.

Could I have saved Jake Garvin? I don't know. Would I do it differently today? Without a doubt. Would it have been easier to accept Jake's death if he had stayed, then killed himself? Certainly not. But at least I would have felt I did everything I could to prevent it instead of having to live with the knowledge that I hid behind rules I already knew to be flawed because I was afraid to be wrong.

Watching and Waiting

Richard Durbin and Valerie Goldner, the quintessential yuppie couple — bright, attractive, successful attorneys, both thirty-four years old, both meticulously turned out and showing the effects of their early-morning fitness regimens. His slim, six-foot frame was draped in an expensive charcoal gray suit, white shirt, red power tie, and tasseled black loafers that virtually sparkled. She was tall, just a few inches shorter than he, slender, and dressed in a dark, well-tailored suit that was saved from severity by a raspberry-colored blouse tied in a bow at the neck. They were an eye-catching twosome, her green-eyed, golden prettiness a striking contrast to his brunet good looks.

There are two chairs (one of them mine) and a couch in my office. The first time they come in, most couples hesitate as they try to figure out how to arrange themselves. Then by common but unspoken consent, they generally sit together on the couch, often close enough to touch, as if by doing so they can ease the conflicts that brought them there. Like the others, Valerie and Richard surveyed the room, but when Valerie seated herself on the couch, Richard unhesitatingly chose the chair a few feet away. She stared at him, confusion and anger written in her eyes. But if he was aware of her feelings, he gave no sign.

I watched quietly, wondering: Is he really so oblivious, so detached from her, or is this willed ignorance? I've seen it often, men who know quite well what their wives or lovers are feeling but feign ignorance, sometimes as a way of avoiding conflict, sometimes because they're so fearful of their own hostility and what it will generate that they can express it only through this kind of passivity. Was Richard one of those passive-aggressive men? I wondered. Although I'm loath to pin a label on a patient because it almost always obscures at least as much as it reveals, it was impossible to keep the thought out of my head.

Valerie's angry words cut through my thoughts. "If you're wondering what we're doing here, I guess you know now. This is typical; just when I need him most to be with me, I mean really *with* me, he backs off." Then, turning to him, "Why, just tell me why you had to start off this way. Why do you have to sit halfway across the room, like we're strangers who don't share a bed?"

He replied calmly, remarking at once on her exaggeration of the distance between them. "I'm not 'halfway across the room.' I can reach over and touch you, see," he said, putting a hand on her knee.

She flicked his fingers away. "It's not good enough, Richard. You know what I mean, but this is what you always do, pick on the one thing I said that's not exactly right and behave as if that's the problem."

Except for greeting them and inviting them into the office, I had not yet said a word. Now, hearing Richard's weary sigh, I stepped in. "*Do* you know what Valerie means?"

He considered my words, a careful response I would soon come to know as characteristic of him. "Yes, I do. I don't know why my sitting here instead of there is creating such a fuss, but I know she thinks I'm distant and go off into my head too much."

"And what do you think?"

"She's probably right, but I don't know if I can change that. I love Val, but I can't always be what she wants."

I sighed inwardly. I'd listened to this dialogue a thousand times before and knew it would go nowhere if we stayed on this plane. So I moved quickly to shift the focus. "Before we get into that," I said, "why don't you tell me something about your-selves so that I can understand how you got here."

Not surprisingly, it was Valerie who spoke up at once while Richard seemed to retreat into some private place, his eyes veiled, his expression unreadable. I listened to her but watched him, puzzled. What was going on inside him? Why did he become so distant so suddenly? But before my thoughts could cohere, Valerie's story called me back. She was in-house counsel for a midsize corporation and was on track to be general counsel when her boss retired sometime in the next few years. She liked her job, was good at what she did, and looked forward to the next step up.

Asked about her family background, she explained that she was born into an upper-middle-class Jewish family and had grown up in a New York City suburb, where her father had a thriving medical practice and her mother was a housewife who wanted more for her daughter. "I knew from the time I was a little girl that I'd be a professional woman; it was my destiny."

Since nothing about her appearance said *Jewish* to me, I remarked about it. Her mother, she said, was born to an Irish Catholic family but had converted to Judiasm to marry her father. "I look like my mother but I'm temperamentally much more like my father, you know that messy emotional Jewish style." She stopped for a moment, as if standing back from her words and weighing their accuracy, then with a laugh, "That's not exactly right because there's nothing calm and quiet about the Irish part of the family either. It's just different."

Valerie and Richard met when her company hired his law firm to defend a lawsuit and he was assigned to the case. She was attracted to him immediately, finding his cool, calm exterior soothing to her more high-strung, easily excitable nature. "I thought it was only on the outside," she said ruefully, "turns out he's not much different on the inside either."

It's an old story — two people who are unconsciously drawn together because each seems to fill a missing part for the other. In this case, he needs her exuberant emotionalism to help him feel alive; she needs his calm steadiness to settle and ground her. I knew nothing yet of Richard's life, but everything about his presentation of self said prototypical WASP. How much, I wondered, does their clash of temperaments owe to their different cultural backgrounds? How much can they change so that they can live together peacefully?

A quiet settled into the room while I waited to see if Richard would respond to Valerie's angry charge. But he seemed lost in his own thought world, so finally I said, "It's your turn, Richard; I'd like to hear your story."

"Good luck," snapped Valerie sarcastically. "If you can get him to tell you about his family, you're a better woman than I am."

He looked at Valerie for a long moment but said nothing. Then turning to me, he said simply, "There isn't a whole hell of a lot to tell. You already know I'm a lawyer. I'm a partner in my firm and, unlike a lot of other lawyers, I don't have any complaints. I work hard, but I'm well rewarded, which is more than most people can say."

"What about your past, your family?"

"Look, this isn't going to get us anywhere," he declared, his voice rising as his calm slipped away. "My family, her family, that's not where the problem lies. Sure, Val and I have different styles, but that didn't create all this stuff between us until she decided she wanted to have a baby. That's the issue, and that's what we should be talking about. She wants a child; I don't. And I'm not going to change my mind about that. Val thinks it's because I have what she calls 'commitment issues,' but it has nothing to do with that. I'll marry her next week, but I won't have children."

Why did he go from cool to hot so quickly? I wondered. And why such certainty? I'd seen plenty of men who were ambivalent about having children, but I'd never heard anyone speak with such heat and conviction.

"You suddenly sound upset and angry, and I wonder what brought that on," I remarked.

He seemed to gather himself together and replied quietly but firmly. "I guess I'm just tired of arguing about it. And I really don't see the point of being here if we're going to sit around for a year talking about our childhoods. The problem is now, and we need help in finding a way to resolve it. We can work out all the other stuff, but how do we get past her obsession with kids?"

Valerie jumped in angrily, "It's not an obsession; it's a normal human desire, and the question is why you hold so stubbornly to your position that you'll never have a child."

"We've been around the park on that one for months," he replied, "and nothing I say makes a dent with you. I don't know what more I can say so that you'll understand."

I intervened. "Perhaps you can make *me* understand, and one way you can do that is to tell me something about your past. There usually are clues back there that help us understand something about our feelings and behavior in the present."

He sat quietly, thoughtful, then, "There really isn't a lot to say. I don't have any family; they're all gone. I grew up in Atlanta. It was an okay family, no big drama, just parents who worked hard and tried to do the best for their kids. I left there when I was seventeen and got a scholarship to college. I haven't been back since."

"You said *kids*, which suggests there were more than just you."

He looked at me curiously, "Do you always pick up on words like that?"

I shrugged. "How many siblings were there?"

"I didn't say there were any."

"Yes, you did; you just didn't say the words aloud."

"I had a brother," he finally admitted reluctantly, "but I haven't seen or talked to him for years; he just disappeared."

"How old were you when your parents died?"

"Look," he said, his voice rising in irritation again. "I don't want to be difficult, but I really don't want to do this. My family isn't the reason I don't want to have children."

I was caught. Do I remark on his irritation, on the obvious fact that it was his way of avoiding something he couldn't or wouldn't talk about? Or do I play it straight and stay with the content he presented? My impulse was to go for the latent stuff, but my fear that I'd lose him altogether if I pushed him too hard too soon stayed my tongue. So I asked simply, "Okay, so what is your reason for not wanting children?"

His reply was a familiar litany of the world's social problems —war, environmental destruction, famine, overpopulation. There were already too many children who should never have been born, he declared. It would be selfish and unjust to bring a new life into such a world, and he would never be a party to it.

Valerie interrupted. "You're right, the world's a shitty place, but I don't see you wanting to exit it."

Wearily, he said, "Christ, Val, we've done this more times than I care to think about. We just keep saying the same things over and over again. What's the point?"

By then I, too, wasn't sure whether there was a point. But Richard had piqued my interest — the absolute certainty with which he spoke about never having children, his avoidance of questions about his family. Was there some secret he was trying to keep, something in his background he feared? Mental illness, perhaps?

But these were questions for the future. Now, as we neared

the end of the session, it was time to evaluate where we'd been and to ask whether they wanted to continue. Valerie was eager to come back; Richard uncertain. "What do you think?" he asked. "Can you help us resolve this?"

"I don't know; it depends at least partly on how much you two *want* to resolve it. And I must say, Richard, you don't leave any room for compromise."

"Since you're not telling her she has to compromise, I guess that means you're on her side."

His comment surprised me, not because it wasn't true but because I didn't think it showed. I *was* more sympathetic with her wish for a child than his refusal to even consider it. I deliberated about what to say for a heartbeat before I realized that only the truth would do. "It's true," I said, "it's easier for me to understand her wish to have a child than your adamant refusal. But that doesn't necessarily mean I'm on her side, or that I think your feelings aren't legitimate, or that I won't be able to understand them if you give me something to work with. And maybe if you can make me understand, it will help Valerie get it as well."

He smiled at that, the first genuine smile I'd seen. "Thanks for telling the truth; I appreciate it. It makes it easier to come back."

I stood at the window watching them cross the street as they went to their separate cars. Years ago when I was new to the practice, I had a consultant who, after hearing my report of a first session, would write the script for what would follow. I would listen in awe and leave feeling inadequate. Would I ever be that good? Now I know that any experienced therapist can make reasonably sound predictions about the course of a therapy, even after a single session. But something told me I was in for some surprises here. Valerie was an open book, but Richard was another story.

In the next few sessions we talked about their relationship, what worked, what didn't, and why. They talked relatively easily at that level and explored their differences without rancor. But no matter how well they handled other problems and conflicts, they were totally stuck on the baby issue. Richard continued to refuse to talk about anything but the present, and I continued to have a nagging sense that there was too much left unsaid for us to make any real progress.

I tried going around his resistance to no effect. I tried confronting it, telling him that his refusal to talk about his past suggested to me that he was hiding something, some secret he thought no one would understand. He replied that he simply had nothing of interest to tell. I insisted that was impossible. "It's in the nature of family life that there's always something interesting to tell." His only answer was "Let it go."

Finally, I suggested that, since Richard didn't want to "bring a new life into the world," perhaps they might consider adopting a child who already was in it and needed a family. Richard thought it a good compromise; Valerie didn't. She'd think about it, she said, if she knew they couldn't have children. But as things stood, adoption wasn't an option, at least not until she could understand why, if he could think about raising someone else's child, it couldn't be theirs.

As the weeks passed, Valerie became angrier, Richard increasingly removed and unwilling to enter the process, and I more exasperated. I hated feeling stuck and incompetent and kept scrutinizing our interactions and myself — my thoughts, my feelings, my motives — and wondering whether I was unconsciously communicating something to Richard that made him unable to trust me?

Finally I could think of nothing more to do. I gave up and spoke my thoughts. "We're stalled, and I've been wondering whether it makes sense for us to continue. My efforts to get past Richard's resistance seem only to make him dig in further, which makes me think that I may not be the best person for you to work with. And I'm not comfortable with continuing to take your money when I don't think I can be helpful."

"You think it's my fault, don't you?"

"Well, I wouldn't put it in terms of 'fault,' but yes, I think your unwillingness to go beyond the surface of things leaves us with nothing left to do."

"Maybe I just can't do what you're asking for."

"I don't believe that; it's why I used the word *unwilling*. I don't know why you won't talk about your past. Maybe something terrible happened then that you don't want to deal with, maybe there's some secret that seems shameful to you, maybe something I can't even guess. But whatever it is I'd put my license to practice on the line to bet that the issue is *won't* not *can't*."

Valerie, who had made a connection with me, was upset at the prospect of giving up, but Richard thought it was a good idea to "take a break." I offered them a referral which both refused. She said, "No, I don't think it's you, it's Richard, and there's no use looking for someone else until he can do what he needs to do, which is to take a good hard look at himself."

"Maybe Val's right about what I need to do, maybe not," Richard answered, "but I agree it's not you. Anyway, I meant it when I said I wanted to take a break; I didn't mean I never wanted to come back. But we've both got a lot to think about, and maybe when we've done that, we'll have more to say."

They left then, leaving me to wonder yet again what I could have done to save the situation. But life and work soon closed in on me, and while I didn't forget them, they weren't in the forefront of my mind in the weeks that followed. Then one day I checked my voice mail to find a message from Richard asking to speak with me. When I returned his call his tension reached out across the phone lines. "I don't know if it's appropriate for me to ask this, but something's happened and I was wondering if I could come in and talk to you."

I hesitated, faced yet again with the difficult decision about whether I ought to see one member of a couple alone. True, I wasn't seeing Richard and Valerie together at the time, and that made a difference. Still, this is one of the no-no's of couples therapy. My family therapy teacher, a man I respected deeply, called it the cardinal sin. Suppose, he would say, you agree to see the husband alone and he confesses an affair. What do you do then? If you keep silent, you collude in deceit and betray the wife, who is also a patient. If you tell, you violate your pledge of confidentiality and the ethical code of your profession. It sounded right to me then, still does. Nevertheless, I've not always followed his teachings, mostly without disastrous results. Mostly, but not always. So I equivocated. "Does Valerie know you're calling?"

"No, and I don't want her to."

His answer did nothing to calm my doubts. "I don't know if I can do this if you're asking me to keep a secret. I think it's better if I refer you to someone else."

His voice broke, "Please, Lillian, don't do this. This is really important; I *need* to see you, and I promise you, it'll be better for Valerie in the long run. I'll tell her, I promise; I'll have no choice. But not right now, not before I can figure a few things out myself."

Secrets never stay secret forever, I thought, certain that he was about to reveal the secret that had blocked our previous work. I was torn between caution and curiosity. "What if I say that my condition for seeing you is that you tell Valerie? I'm not saying you have to tell her what's troubling you, only that you want to come in and talk to me."

"I don't know; I'll have to think about it."

"Let's both think about it overnight and talk tomorrow."

At ten o'clock that evening there was a message from Richard asking me to call "any time." He picked up the phone on the first ring. "I told Val that I called you, and she's fine with it. Actually, more than fine; she really thinks it's great. Do you have some time tomorrow?"

Between his urgency and my curiosity, I didn't have to think long about finding him an hour.

He looked worn when he arrived the next day, as if he hadn't slept much for a while. "You look tired," I remarked as he settled into a chair.

"It's been a hard couple of days," he said in a voice choked with anguish, then fell silent while he tried to pull himself together. He ran his hands through his hair, grasped the back of his head as if to hold it in place, and made several unsuccessful attempts to speak. Finally, he burst out, "Christ, where do I begin? You know, you take a step, you do something, and you don't necessarily think when you're doing it that it leads to the next step and the next, and before you know it, you're irreversibly committed to something you didn't fully intend."

"Nothing's irreversible in this life, Richard, except maybe death."

"Oh God, how I wish you were right."

He wept then, bitter wrenching sobs that racked his body and soul. I waited quietly, not wanting to disturb the moment. "I can't hold on to it anymore; I just can't do it," he cried between sobs.

I moved closer and put my hand on his arm. "You don't have to. Whatever it is, it can't be so bad that it can't be fixed."

He lifted his head then, his face ravaged, and rubbed his eyes fiercely as if to wipe away the evidence of his tears. "I've never done that in my whole life," he apologized.

"Then it was too long in coming."

He tried to smile. "Thank you. I can't make up my mind whether you're tough or kind."

"Maybe because, like most people, I can be both."

I waited, knowing he would speak when he was ready. We all write our own biographies, framing the narrative in ways that are congruent with the self we know and the one we want to be. It isn't that we lie to ourselves and to others, only that there are many ways to interpret and assemble the facts of our lives.

So, for example, a woman who suffered some traumatic event like incest or rape can tell the story two ways. In one version it's the central fact of her life, the one she can never forget and never get past. It's a story of victimization that builds on itself until it defines who she is and what she can do. In another account it's a terrible event that marked her life but not her identity. It's a tale of transcendence in which the past isn't denied or forgotten; it simply doesn't form the core of the narrative she has constructed.

How we write the script depends on who we are and how we internalize the events of our world. Obviously, some stories are more psychologically functional than others. But every story changes with time, not just because memories grow dim but because we ourselves change, and the story we need to tell us where we've been and who we are now is different today than it was yesterday. It's when the tale remains fixed that therapy can be most effective by helping us to reframe the narrative to focus on change rather than stasis, on strength rather than weakness.

Minutes passed during which I could almost see Richard trying to frame his thoughts, to find a way to tell his story that made sense to himself as well as to me. Finally, he spoke. "You were right; there's a secret I've kept since I was seventeen. I feel like I've been watching and waiting my whole life since then to be found out, and now here it is, the accounting I've been dreading all these years.

"Do you have any idea what it's like to have to be vigilant every minute, to watch everything you say and do, never to be able to relax and just be, to wait and wait and wait, knowing it all has to come to an end, but never knowing when and how? Any idea what that means?"

I couldn't respond; I was too busy trying to catch the thoughts that flew through my mind. Was he trying to tell me what I thought he was saying? Could he be passing? A black man passing as white? Was this why he was so adamant about not wanting children? I looked at him more closely. No, there was no sign, no feature that would mark him as anything but a white man.

Earlier in my life, long before I became a therapist, I'd worked in the black community, had many black friends, and heard plenty of "passing" stories. Later, in my clinical practice, I saw a couple of patients who'd gone that route and suffered the consequences. The words Richard spoke, the feelings he talked about, I'd heard them before.

"You don't have any idea what I'm talking about, do you?"

"Maybe, I'm not sure, so why not just say it."

He tried, but he seemed to choke on the words. He sat back in the chair, exhausted, one hand covering his face. His pain filled the room and became too much to bear silently. Several times he tried to speak but the words wouldn't come. Finally, I took his free hand and, speaking as quietly and gently as I knew how, said them for him. "Richard, are you trying to tell me you're passing?"

He looked at me, then, relief spreading across his tormented features, and nodded assent. Someone else finally knew, said the words, and the world hadn't shifted on its axis. I had been so involved in observing him that I hadn't noticed the tension in my own body until I felt it begin to slip away as the charged atmosphere in the room relaxed.

"I'm so ashamed," he wept, "so ashamed."

I was silent, preoccupied with my own feelings, remembering what it felt like to feel such shame. Why is it that our patients seem unerringly to push us back into a confrontation with our own unresolved issues? I'm not much of a believer in paraspsychology, but I have to admit that at times like these I wonder: Do we choose each other because we know, in some other way of knowing, that we share bonds of understanding? It was a fanciful thought, but one that distracted me for a moment from the painful memories of the time many years ago when I, too, was passing. Not a black living as white, but a Jew living as a Gentile.

I was fifteen, had just graduated from high school, and needed a job to help support my family. Since I was a pretty kid with good secretarial skills, I looked like someone who would be easy to place. So I was greeted warmly when I walked into an employment agency, asked to fill out an application, and assured there were jobs available. But it was still legal then for employment applications to inquire about religion, and time after time the welcoming smile turned icy as soon as the woman I was speaking with saw the word *Jewish*.

Each time the promise of a job vanished before my pained and bewildered eyes, I left feeling angry, humiliated, and helpless. Finally, after repeatedly bumping up against the same warm reception followed by a chilly rejection, I changed my surname and wrote *Protestant* in the box that called for religion. The next day I had a job.

For a while after I declared myself a Protestant, I was fascinated by my new identity, by the pretense that I wasn't an outsider, a member of a stigmatized minority. It was seductive to be one of "them," the alien other, to know what it felt like to be part of the majority, to be someone who could take her place in the world for granted. There were moments when I could actually believe I was what I pretended to be. But they were short-lived.

There was too much to hide, too many lies, too many times when I had to listen silently to anti-Semitic remarks — nothing terrible, no fulminating hatred, just the kinds of comments that were hurtful precisely because they reflected stereotypes that were so taken for granted, so deeply ingrained in my workmates' consciousness that they went unnoticed. I learned that a name isn't just a name; it's part of how you know yourself, part of your past, your community, your heritage. Give away your name, and some part of your self goes with it.

I was in a daily confrontation with myself, caught between the shame of another lie, another betrayal of myself and my people, and the fact that I needed and wanted to work. Within a year the strain of passing became intolerable. I quit my job, took back my name, and with it the remnants of my self-respect.

Now, hearing Richard's story, I thought there's always a "good" reason for such lies, his perhaps better than mine, since it's so much harder to be black than Jewish in this society. But the shame that accompanies the deception lives well beyond the act itself, a lesson I learned yet again as Richard's anguish brought back my own.

My thoughts shifted from me to him. If it was so hard for me to live with myself for one year, what must it have been like for him? Seventeen years during which he cut himself off from his past and everyone in it; years when he couldn't own crucial parts of himself, when he found out what it was like to be truly alone; years of lies and hiding, even with the woman he loved; years of feeling like a fraud because he was one.

I've had many patients who lived in secret shame, accomplished men and women who were plagued by the belief that their achievements were undeserved, some kind of a fluke, a con they'd somehow managed to perpetrate on those around them; women and men who lived with the anxiety that one day they would be found out as the frauds they felt themselves to be. It's a difficult fear to treat because it's buried so deeply into the patient's core sense of himself, but common enough so that there's a name for the suffering: *the imposter syndrome.* But this was different, someone who felt like a fraud with good reason.

Richard's tormented voice jolted me out of my memories, and I dragged my mind back into the room. "What will I do? How can I tell Val? How am I going to face all the people I've lied to all these years?"

"We'll deal with that," I assured him with more certainty than I felt. How does one deal with unraveling a life and all the lies that went into constructing it? For me it was easy. I could leave my job and never see any of those people again. And even if the truth had come out, I was white, a distinct advantage even for a Jew. But what happens when a woman finds out that the man she plans to marry is black? Even if the racial issues aren't paramount, how does she deal with the betrayal of trust? But all I could say right then was "Let's take it one step at a time. Right now I need to understand why this is coming up for you at this time."

I hadn't realized that I was still holding his hand until he pulled it away and covered his face again. Then, his voice muffled as he spoke into his hands, he said, "My sister came to see me at my office; I had no idea she knew where I was. She came to tell me my mother had died."

A sister he'd never mentioned; a mother he'd led me to believe was dead! "I think you better tell me the story from the beginning, starting with your family."

It was a familiar tale. His father worked sporadically at one of the low-level jobs that were available to poorly educated black men, and his mother was a cook for a wealthy white family. When they were both working, the house was relatively peaceful. But as the years went on, his father worked less and drank more, and the conflict between the parents spilled over into brutality against the children.

Richard was the youngest of three children, the one who was different, who was bright, eager to learn, liked school, and was good at it. He was the child most clearly destined for something more than the life his parents led and, therefore, the one most likely to generate his father's envy and feel his wrath.

Not only was he different from his parents and siblings, he *looked* different. In a family where hair was kinky and skin color ranged from café au lait to deep brown, Richard had "good" hair, and looked white, a matter of pride to his light-skinned mother. But in a community acutely attuned to the quality of hair and the shadings of skin color, where light skin and "good" hair are among the most highly valued characteristics, his whiteness, and his mother's pleasure in it, was an affront to his dark-skinned father.

Richard's brother, four years older than he, was "the tough kid on the street," didn't have much use for his younger brother, and often used him "as a punching bag." His sister, who was three years his senior, was "off in her own world," and they had little in common.

By the time he was in fourth grade, he knew that his way out was through school, and his father's rage — the endless taunts, the beatings — only increased his determination to escape the family, the community, and the life he saw there. His mother encouraged and supported her son's aspirations and, in the early years, tried to protect him from his father's wrath. But she was no match for her husband, and her interventions usually left her as battered and bruised as Richard was. "I guess eventually she decided there was nothing she could do," said Richard, "so she gave up and just tried to stay out of his way. I never forgave her for not stopping the son of a bitch. What kind of a mother lets someone do those things to her kid?"

"One who feels helpless, I imagine," I replied.

He snorted. "Helpless is a little kid being beaten up by his drunken father while his mother looks the other way, that's helpless."

When he was seventeen he finally got what he wanted — a ticket out of the family in the form of a scholarship to an Ivy League university. "Once I left, I never looked back, not even when my father died, which happened during my first year away. When I first heard he was dead, all I could think of was that the bastard lost his reason for living when I wasn't around for him to torment. But actually he was killed in a drunken brawl, which is just what he deserved."

Despite his mother's request, he refused to go home for the funeral. After months of living in another world, of finding himself around people with whom he shared some common ground for the first time in his life, all he wanted was to forget the life he left behind. "Do you have any idea what it's like," he asked, "to live in a family where you're a total outsider, like this whole thing is some kind of a mistake, one of those mix-ups where they give the kid to the wrong family?

"It wasn't any different outside, either; I look white, for God's sake. How do you think that went over with the kids on the street? Or with the people at church, for that matter? Then after all those years you suddenly find yourself in a place where there are other people like you. There was no way I could go back."

His words washed over me and left me momentarily silent as they scratched at a very old scar and drew some blood. Yes, I wanted to say, I know just what it's like to live in a family where you feel like an alien, a visitor from another planet. But it was his story that was important right then, not mine. So I nudged him on. "When did you decide to pass?"

"I didn't decide; it just happened. People at school thought I was white, and at first it was like a joke. You know, a kid saying, 'Yeah, let's see what this scene is like.' This was the early seventies; there weren't a lot of black students on campus, and those who were there hung together like they were stuck to each other. I didn't feel any special affinity for them, and I don't know if they even knew I was black. You know, black people know sometimes when whites don't. Whatever, we never came toward each other."

Nothing "just happens," of course. Richard's inaction was itself an action. But I listened quietly to his tale of the slide from black to white. There was no defining moment, just an incremental process: one small step taken, then another; one lie told, and the next, and the next; one assumption after another left unchallenged. "I just let it happen, and there it was: I was white. It was so easy and so seductive. You just stepped into the role and you went from being a member of a minority nobody liked to one of the majority, somebody they wanted to know.

"But when you start something like that, you don't realize what you're getting into. I didn't count on all the lies I'd have to tell, or on how I'd spend my life being vigilant, watching and waiting to be found out. And with all that, I never felt like I belonged anyway. How could I? They were a bunch of privileged white kids whose idea of a hard time was not getting to sleep with the girl they wanted. Maybe I would have had more common ground with the black kids on campus, but I doubt it. They were so fundamentally black; I mean, that was their identity.

"Me? I didn't know who or what I was. I knew I wasn't white, but I didn't feel black. It was like living in no-man's land. Talk about the man without a country; I was it. There was no place to stand I could call my own, never was."

"I know it's hard," I sympathized, "especially when you're a child, to feel so marginalized in your world. But in adulthood I believe it can be an asset. If you don't really belong anywhere, you're freer to find your own way and not as likely to get pushed into the kind of conformity that stifles creativity."

"Easy for you to say," he retorted bitterly.

The self-pity I heard in his words troubled me. Should I let him know he wasn't the only one in the room with a sad story? Would it help to put his experience in some larger perspective? After a moment's thought, I decided he needed a jolt and replied, "No, not easy. I learned the lesson the hard way, just as I hope you will."

He looked surprised, hesitated, trying to decide whether to pursue the subject. Then, "You look like anything but a marginal woman to me."

"But it isn't the outside, is it? If I were to make some guesses about you from the outside, as I did when we first met, I'd assume you were the quintessential WASP, the guy for whom everything came easily."

He laughed at that, a sound without joy, and asked, "So will you tell me it's none of my business if I ask why you feel marginal?"

I was relieved at this sign that he could think of something beside himself and the problems that faced him. It seemed useful to answer his question, if only so he could see the possibilities that might lie ahead for him. The question, at such a moment, however, is always what and how much to tell.

Psychotherapy has no immunity from the trends in the wider culture. Consequently, as our society has become more open and self-revealing, a movement has arisen in some psychological circles that calls for a similar openness between therapist and patient. It's an advance over the old notions of the therapist as a neutral blank screen onto which a patient projects her neurotic transference fantasies on a near-silent presence. Among other things, it recognizes that there are two thinking, feeling people in the room whose interaction affects the feelings and behaviors of both of them.

But as is the case with a theoretical advance in a field where practice is fluid and technique depends upon the individuals and the circumstances involved, it's impossible to teach someone precisely how to put theory into practice. Each therapist, therefore, is left to figure out the delicate balance with only the haziest guidelines. Not surprisingly, the result is a jumble where some get it right; others, fearful of overstepping the bounds, say too little; while still other more adventuresome souls burden their patients with revelations that are inappropriate and stories they don't need to hear.

"You're not here to listen to my life story," I replied, "but I certainly think you have a right to know some things about me. So you want to know how I know about being marginal? The short answer is the same way you do. By the time I was five, I knew I didn't belong in the family I was given. My mother knew it, too, maybe even before I did, and it made her as angry as your father was, with the same result. I got out by marrying, which is what a girl of my generation and class did. But that had its own problems, which we'll save for another day."

"I guess you never know, do you?" he remarked in wonder.

"You think you have people figured out, then they're not at all what you thought. I had you figured for someone who grew up with a silver spoon." He was silent for a few seconds, thinking about the contradiction between his perception and reality, then, his dark eyes filled with warmth and caring, he said gently, "Thanks for telling me; it makes a difference to know you're right there with me."

By then we had talked for more than two hours, and we were both spent, so I suggested he come back the next day. He was beset with questions: What would he do between now and then? How could he go to work as if nothing happened? What would he say to Valerie who would surely ask about this visit?

We agreed that he'd take a few days off from work and ask Valerie to bear with him until he was ready to talk, then set up another two-hour session for the next day. I watched him go, relieved to have the respite but anxious and uncertain about where to go from here. Getting the confession was one thing. How to help him get through the next weeks when he was "coming out" as black was quite another. Worse yet, what did I have to say to a man who was about to exchange the privilege of whiteness for the most despised of American identities — blackness?

I felt awed by the responsibility. Maybe he would have been better off with his secret intact? But that was my anxiety speaking; I really knew better. The secret was revealed because its time had come, because few secrets are really forever, and because such secrets inevitably distort the internal life of those who try to hold them.

We spent the next two weeks in daily meetings, sorting over his past and trying to find a way into the future. He talked about his abandonment of his family as he had about passing. "It wasn't a decision; it just happened, a piece at a time."

It seemed to me he wouldn't be able to come to terms with

what he'd done without acknowledging that he'd done it, without understanding that his behavior wasn't an accident but had been fueled by a complicated set of feelings about his family, about himself, about a society that treated its African American citizens unjustly, about the cost of being black and the certain knowledge that by becoming white he guaranteed himself a different and easier life than the one he'd known. So I assured him that nothing "just happens," that he'd made a choice when he allowed himself to pass from black to white. True, the fact that he looked white, and that others assumed it, made it possible for him to pass. But the decision to live out the charade was his, and having made it, he couldn't sustain the life he'd chosen and remain in contact with his family. How do you live white and show up with a black mother?

He wrestled with my words, fought with me at first. "It's easy for you to judge me, but what the hell do you know about what it's like?" he asked, his eyes blazing. "Christ, everybody assumed I was white. What should I have done, spent my life setting the record straight? Or just go with it? Do you have any idea what it's like to watch the whole world change right before your eyes just because they think you're white? What would you have done?"

"I don't know." I replied honestly, "But I know the temptation to join the privileged mainstream world because I tried it once."

My words shocked him into a silent, questioning stare. I told him then about changing my name and presenting myself to the world as a Christian. "I know it's different and a lot easier going from Jew to Gentile than from black to white," I assured him. "And even though my 'transformation' wasn't as complete as yours, I know very well what you mean when you speak of always watching and waiting to be found out."

It was several minutes after I finished speaking before he

could find words. When he spoke he gave voice to the very question, albeit not in the same language, I'd asked myself earlier. "How did I ever find you? Do you suppose God sent me here?" he asked, tears streaming down his face.

We spent the next weeks talking about shame, the shame of his own stigmatized heritage and the shame of abandoning it, the shame of knowing he was a fraud and the self-hatred that accompanied it. They were wrenching sessions for us both, lived in the spirit of two people who had been to the same hell. He wept and raged and wondered where it would all end. "Who the hell am I? I can't live in the white world anymore, and I don't even know how to be black."

I relived my own past, realizing as I did that Richard wasn't the only one who had to confront the choices he'd made more honestly. True, I became a Christian because I couldn't get a job as a Jew, but others who faced the same discriminatory practices found other ways around it. I felt again the self-hating anti-Semitism that had seeped into my soul when I was still a child, bringing with it the shame of my mother's foreign accent, the wish that she wouldn't talk so no one would know she was a Jewish immigrant. I recalled the exhilaration I felt when I first walked through the world as a Gentile, the relief it brought from the burden of being Jewish. And I understood more clearly than ever how large a part my own Jewish self-hatred played in my decision to assume a counterfeit identity.

While Richard and I struggled with questions of identity and choice, Valerie stood in the wings getting restive as she watched Richard's suffering and his increasing withdrawal into a world she couldn't see. She had a right to know what was going on, she told him, and I agreed with her. The question was only how and when. He was tormented, certain that she would leave him, that her wish for a child with him would evaporate when she understood it might be black. "How do I do it? What do I say?" Finally, knowing he couldn't put it off any longer, he said, "I can't do it alone; I need you there."

We met on a Saturday, the only time when I could set aside as much time as they might need without other obligations intruding. Haltingly, Richard told Valerie the truth, each word wrenched from him with an effort that was painful to watch. She sat unmoving, white with shock. As her silence grew, he began frantically to try to explain, but there was too much to say, too much he couldn't yet explain to himself, too much for her to hear. She looked like a statue, silent, her body posture rigid, her eyes blank and uncomprehending. I prodded, "Can you say something, Valerie?"

Slowly, as if she couldn't get her tongue around the words, she replied, "I don't understand." Then without another word, she got up and left the office, pushing off Richard's attempts to follow her. At about eleven o'clock that night, he called. "Val still hasn't come home."

By the next morning anger replaced shock. Valerie stormed into their apartment and told Richard to move out. It was bad enough to live such a lie in the outside world, she exclaimed, but they had shared a home and a bed for over a year, and he never once let slip a clue, not even when she asked question after question about his past, his home, his family. How could she ever trust him again? Did he even know truth from lies anymore? No apology, no plea, no request for time and talk moved her.

The loss devastated Richard. It was weeks before he could face the anxiety of taking the next step: coming out to the people he worked with. But he understood that once Valerie knew his secret, it was no longer secure. Finally, he gathered the courage and went to the managing partner of his firm, a man who had been his mentor when he first arrived. "It was like a bolt out of the blue," Richard reported. "He looked at me for a long time and couldn't say a word. It was like Val all over again. Then finally he said he needed time to think about it and would get back to me. Nothing else, just that."

Two days later he informed Richard that he had called a partners' meeting for the end of the day and expected him to be there to tell his story. Richard called me in a panic. "If this is what I got from Ron, it'll be a disaster with the others."

I could only imagine what it would cost him to face thirty-two colleagues, men and women who had trusted that they knew him, and recount the tale of his deception. But all I could offer was the hope that people are sometimes more generous than we expect them to be, along with the reminder that he'd already been through the worst.

His colleagues listened, asked questions, told him they were distressed and angry, and adjourned until the next night when they would vote on what to do. The next morning, certain that they'd vote against him, he tendered his resignation to the managing partner who refused to accept it. When the votes were counted later in the day, there were a few dissenters but most were in favor of asking him to stay.

Richard was grateful but anxious. What would it be like to work with these people now that they knew he'd lied to them? "People talk," he said, and he didn't "relish being the hot topic at the water cooler." How could he gain their trust again? Did he even want to? Maybe he should just quit and start anew somewhere else, perhaps even in another city where no one knew his history and he could come to them as a black man? "A white black man," he amended bitterly. "It's like God's bad joke, isn't it?"

I was the voice of caution, trying to hold him in place, to keep his emotional temperature in check so that he wouldn't make decisions he might regret later. As the immediate turmoil of his life subsided, it wasn't hard to convince him to hold any big decisions in abeyance until he could consider all options more clearly.

Richard and I continued to work together for the next two years, painfully grueling sessions at first where he despaired of finding a way to live while he climbed the various internal and external hurdles that awaited him. He sifted and sorted through the narrative he'd developed until then, came to understand himself and what he'd done more fully, and began slowly to find ways to own being black while not losing his foothold in the white world with all its perks.

"Will I ever get it all right?" he asked one day.

I smiled. "If you do, you'll be the first person ever to have done so."

"But you did," he protested.

I laughed at that and told him about the patient who likened therapy to bread being baked in an oven and who every now and then asked if she was baked yet. "It doesn't work that way," I told Richard. "No one is ever fully baked because life is a process that continually confronts us with new challenges that require new adaptations. The only way out of that bind is to be dead, either literally or metaphorically."

"Some help you are," he quipped. "I thought you therapists taught people how to be happy."

"It's a false promise; the best we can do is to the give you the tools to deal with what life throws at you."

About six months after she left him Valerie came back into Richard's life, tentatively at first, unsure about what was possible between them. She had spent a lot of time, she told him, asking herself how much of her anger was because of his deception, how much born of the simple fact that he was black and her own unacknowledged feelings about an interracial marriage. "She could be all for it in the abstract," Richard reported, "but she seems to have found out some things about herself once I came out."

After about three months of meeting, talking, testing, Valerie realized that, through all the anger and pain, she had never stopped loving Richard and asked him to move back in, which he did happily. The question of marriage and children arose quickly, but now the tables were turned. With his secret out, Richard's resistance to having a child melted away, and he was eager to marry and start a family. But Valerie hesitated, caught between her love for Richard, her desire for a child, and her fear that she might not be up to raising a biracial child, a child who quite possibly wouldn't resemble either of its parents.

At Valerie's insistence Richard reestablished a relationship with his sister, not a close one, too much had happened to separate them, but enough so that they could meet from time to time, get to know her husband and children, and to learn how his brother ended up serving a life sentence for murder. For Richard it meant a connection with his past that with time he came to value. For Valerie it was both a way to test herself in an alien environment that might soon be hers and to understand something about Richard and where he came from that made him seem less opaque.

With time Valerie was able to quiet her fears enough to marry Richard. A year later their baby was born, a lovely coffee-and-cream-colored little girl.

"People still assume I'm white," Richard reported one day, "and when they see Gina, they figure she's adopted. But now I don't have to think about how to crack into their assumptions anymore. I just tell them she's my natural child. It gets some I-don't-believe-it stares," he chuckled, "but at least I'm telling it like it is."

Border Crossings

The case conference is one of the cornerstones of clinical training and practice. For those new to the field, it's a place to hear firsthand the work of senior therapists. For the more experienced, it's the only public forum, the one place where their work is subject to scrutiny by colleagues, the one also where the collective wisdom and experience of their peers is available to them.

It was conference day at the clinic where I was working, and Marianne Archer, a staff psychiatrist, had just presented the case of Ms. O. (To maintain confidentiality a patient's name is never used.) "It's not just the panic attacks that concern me," she concluded. "I see distinctly paranoid features as well."

The patient, a twenty-three-year-old college senior, had been brought into the clinic in the throes of a severe panic attack. She was hospitalized briefly while being stabilized on medication, then released with the recommendation that she enter therapy. She was distinctly unenthusiastic about the idea.

A few days later she came back, complaining that while the drug soothed the panic somewhat, it left her so lethargic and disoriented that she could barely function. Marianne was reluctant to, as we say in the trade, "become a med stop," partly because it's not what she trained for, but mostly because she believed, as most therapists do, that drugs alone don't do the job. So after adjusting Ms. O's medication, she urged her again to consider therapy, explaining that while drugs were useful in helping her through the crisis period, they were most effective in the long term when used in conjunction with psychotherapy. After much hesitation, Ms. O reluctantly agreed.

It was now several months later and Marianne, an experienced therapist who supervised trainees at the clinic, found herself stymied before Ms. O, a patient she characterized as "stubbornly resistant and decidedly paranoid. She reacts as if I'm trying to take something from her when I ask a question."

The facts, as Marianne conveyed them, were clear: Ms. O was the second of four children, the single mother of a daughter born when she was sixteen years old. Her pregnancy was a scandal in her Mexican American family, but as practicing Catholics, abortion wasn't an option. Although her father threatened at first to throw her out of the house, his wife's calmer response prevailed, and after a while, even he stood by his daughter.

Seven years later Ms. O still lived in her parents' home, where her mother and younger sister had helped raise her daughter while she finished high school. Although she also had worked part-time, she graduated near the top of her class and was awarded a full scholarship to the university, the only one of her siblings to go beyond high school.

The narrow confines of family and community in which she'd been raised began to fall away at college, and she reached out eagerly for the offerings laid before her. She was an excellent and committed student, garnering a 3.8 grade point average. During her junior year, she caught the attention of one of her professors, who encouraged her studies and suggested that she consider graduate school. The following year she applied and, with the strong support of her mentor and two other faculty members, was accepted to the graduate program in Latin American history. A few weeks later, she fell into the panic attack that brought her into the clinic.

It's heady stuff to be singled out like that. Heady and anxiety-provoking, I thought as the memory of my own experience of being "chosen" came flooding back. For I, too, had been picked out of the crowd by a professor who saw potential I didn't know I had and encouraged me onto a path I hadn't ever thought of. It was hard to listen, to push past the tumult in my mind as I relived the wonder and the fear: the thrill of being chosen, the excitement of hearing a respected professor tell me I was smart enough to get a Ph.D., the anxiety the idea generated, the fear that I'd be found wanting.

I was a grown woman when that happened, one who had climbed out of the working class years before, a woman who had lived half a lifetime and had had a successful career before I gave it up to become a college freshman at age thirty-nine. If I was caught in so much conflict, how much harder must it be for a twenty-three-year-old Mexican American woman from a working-class family to find herself on the brink of an unknown world?

The case and its puzzles generated a lively discussion as the therapists gathered around the table asked questions, offered suggestions, speculated, and theorized. I listened with increasing frustration. I not only knew from personal experience the costs of crossing class borders, I'd studied it and written about it. Moreover, since I had a doctorate in sociology before I became a psychotherapist, the psychological issues raised by differences in class, race, and ethnicity were never far from my mind. But no one, neither Marianne nor anyone else in the room, seemed to see significance in the fact that Ms. O had grown up in a Latino working-class family. Instead, the conversation was totally focused on her internal dynamics: on her relationships in the family, on the primitive nature of her anxiety, on the possibility that her panic was a response to some repressed experience.

After listening quietly for a while, I suggested that there might be a connection between Ms. O's panic attacks and her class and cultural background. "The prospect of crossing over into the professional middle class, a place where she would never feel the comfort of community that surrounded her in the barrio where she lived, could well be daunting enough to send her into a panic."

Marianne listened thoughtfully, then replied, "But she made that choice long ago when she put her feet on the path toward college and graduate school."

"True," I said, "but then it was only a dream, and probably not a well-articulated one at that. Facing the reality, with all it implies about loss of the past, fear of the future, and anxiety about her own adequacy, could certainly leave her conflicted enough to generate panic."

There was a moment of silence as people thought about our exchange, then one of the other therapists joined in. "Even if everything you say is right, it doesn't sufficiently explain the patient's idiosyncratic response. Millions of other Americans make the same transition without panic attacks. Anyway, moving up is what we're expected to do; that's what this country is all about," he concluded dismissively.

His tone angered me, but I learned long ago that neither outrage nor a raised voice change minds. Worse yet, I knew if I spoke with the passion that was rising in me I'd become the subject of their inquiry into my "countertransference" and "over-identification" with the patient. So I took a deep breath and spoke with a calm I didn't feel.

I agreed that anxiety about crossing class and cultural borders wasn't the only explanation for Ms. O's panic, but I also said that we couldn't understand her experience without taking account of what this passage meant to her. I talked about how hard it is for parents who are caught between their pride in their upwardly mobile children and their pain as they see them moving inexorably out of the family orbit and into a distant world. And for the children who have to go it alone. "Ms. O," I said, "is caught in a no-win bind. If she takes the path before her, it will be a lonely one; there's no educated middle-class family or community to lend support. If she retreats, she consigns herself to a life she now knows is smaller than the one she can have."

My remarks made little impact, partly because I was speaking of a culture and a way of life that was far from their experience. But the more important reason, I believe, lies in psychology itself. For despite the fact that in recent years mental health professionals of all stripes have sought to become more aware of cultural differences and the way they affect individual psychology, the basis of psychological theory still lies in the inner world of the individual and in the assumption that there are psychological universals that are independent of broad social and cultural differences. So while more practitioners than before now see race and ethnicity (class differences are still almost wholly out of their vision) as significant factors in a patient's life, there's little support in the theory for integrating these new understandings into practice. Therefore, the primary focus of most therapies remains on the patient's internal dynamics.

It's true, of course, that therapy must be concerned with how a person internalizes the external world, how he takes it in and processes it in his own unique way. But for most therapists, as for Freud, the starting point is inside, not outside. So, for example, for Freud, religion and the belief in a god is the externalization, the projection, if you will, of the internal need for a father protector. Compare that with Marx, who argued that religion is a social institution devised by an elite to control the masses.

Each articulated a significant truth while also failing to grasp the other side. The result lives with us today: Psychologists still have trouble granting an independent role to social phenomena in the making of psychological problems. Marxist theorists still fail to understand either the psychological need that underlies belief or the fact that, even if that need is manufactured by social manipulation as they claim, once internalized it develops a life and force of its own. In the real world, religious belief is a response to a need for certainty, order, and protection, as Freud would have it, and religion as expressed in the institutional church is, indeed, an instrument of social control, as Marx would argue.

I left the conference feeling disgruntled, out of place, and unable to get Ms. O's story out of my mind. Was I overreacting? Too identified with the patient? Maybe. I'd been there; I knew what she was feeling. I'd paid the price of upward mobility: the uncertainty about my abilities, the anxiety, the sense of isolation, the lack of a shared vocabulary with those from my past, my family's anger as they saw me moving further and further away, the sense of always being marginal in both worlds, even after all these years.

But it wasn't my case, and as the days flew by, Ms. O and her trials fell out of my consciousness. Then about a month later the clinic director asked to see me. Marianne, he told me, had a family emergency and was taking an extended leave of absence. Could I take over some of her cases? I wasn't thrilled at the prospect because I was already on overload. But I knew it wasn't really a question when he handed me three case files before the question mark made it to the end of the sentence.

I took the files back to my office, looked at them only to see when the patients were due in again, and put them aside until I had time to digest them. The next day, I scanned the first two files and saw nothing special to claim my attention in either of them. But the third, Delfina Ortega, brought me up short. This was Ms. O, the woman Marianne had presented at the case conference.

I wondered if I caught the case by accident or design? The director never said a word during the discussion of the case, but he generally tended to be somewhat more clinically adventurous than his staff. I assumed, therefore, that the assignment hadn't been made randomly, an assumption he confirmed when I ran into him in the hall later that day and asked about it. "You were itching for it; you got it," he said with a smile. "Now go for it."

A few days later, I stood in the doorway of the waiting room taking in Delfina Ortega's physical presence. She sat in a corner, a small, slightly square person hunched over a book, a Hi-Liter pencil at the ready as her eyes scanned the page. There was no missing her Mexican Indian ancestry, from her body type to her straight jet black hair and her deep olive-toned skin. It can't be easy for her, I thought as I approached, to enter a world in which she looks so different from most of the people around her. She looked up as I neared, her black eyes questioning my presence, but she remained still. I reached out to shake her hand as I introduced myself. She took my hand limply but continued to sit quietly as if waiting for something.

I realized that no one had told her that Marianne couldn't be there, so I apologized for the oversight and invited her to come with me to my office where we could talk about it. She stood then and followed me down the hall, still without a word.

As soon as the door closed behind her, she turned to me and asked sullenly, "Where's the other one?"

"The other one!" Do I pass over that or mark it? I decided to comment. "No name, huh? Guess you must be plenty mad at her."

I was rewarded with a thin smile.

I explained that Marianne was on leave and that we would be working together from then on. She shrugged as if neither

Marianne nor I were of any consequence. "I don't really want to be here."

"Then why do you come?"

"Because she said she wouldn't give me the pills if I didn't."

Surprised, I replied, "You can stop coming any time you want to. If the medication is helping, I'll be glad to see that someone here continues to prescribe it."

"You mean it?"

I assured her I did, then sat quietly waiting to see what she would do or say. She was silent, too, looking around the room as if to see what it would tell her. Her eyes fell on a painting of a grandmother holding a child protectively in her arms, one of a collection by Mexican artists that my husband and I had accumulated over the years. I watched her look from it to me, puzzled.

"That's a Coronel," she said, sounding as if she couldn't quite believe it. "I took a course in Mexican art last year and saw slides of his work. The colors, they're beautiful but dark, not like a lot of Mexican paintings."

"*Se llama La Abuela,*" I said. (He calls it *The Grandmother.*)

"*Habla español?*" she asked excitedly. (Do you speak Spanish?)

"*Es lástima, pero hablo solamente un poquito.*" (It's a pity, but I speak only a very little.)

We talked for a while, just two women in conversation trying to mine the common ground we'd just discovered. She wanted to know how I learned Spanish. I told her I studied it at college and had kept it up reasonably well during the years when I traveled to Mexico fairly regularly. But it had been some time since I had done that, and my skills had atrophied. She asked how I came to have the Coronel. I told her that my husband and I had collected Mexican art in the early years of our marriage and that our walls at home were filled with those paintings.

She forgot where she was for a minute and, speaking like an excited child, asked, "Oh, can I see them sometime?"

I knew I'd lose her if responded in some way that shamed her for asking, and I also knew I couldn't give her a simple yes. So I spoke carefully, looking for words that were positive but that left the options open. "I love to show the collection to someone who appreciates Mexican art, but I think it's time for us to talk about you."

"Isn't it all in there?" she asked, pointing to the file.

"Yes, it is, but there's a lot left to talk about, like how it feels to be the only one in your family to go to college."

She shrugged. "It's okay. Why wouldn't it be okay?"

"I didn't say it wasn't okay; I only asked how it feels."

She looked at me speculatively, as if trying to decide how much to say, then in an almost reflexive response, her body spoke for her as she folded her arms across her chest and retreated to silence.

We were close to the end of the session, and it didn't seem the moment to push her, so I turned instead to the logistics of our next meeting. That done, I told her I was glad to have met her and had enjoyed our conversation about Mexican art.

She looked surprised. Her body posture, so rigid a moment before, relaxed a bit as she rose and headed for the door. Then, just as she was about to close it behind her, she turned back and said, "*Me gusta la pintura porque ella me recuerda de mi madre y mi hija. Hasta la vista.*" (I like the painting because it reminds me of my mother and my daughter. So long.) And with that she was gone.

She was measurably more at ease when she arrived for our next session and was hardly settled in her seat before she launched into a soliloquy about how hard she was working at school, offering "evidence" of how difficult it was for her, about how much she didn't know, would never know. "I'm so far behind, I'll never be able to catch up," she concluded.

I started to speak, but she interrupted before I uttered a word. "I know, I know," she said, her words tumbling out impatiently. "You're thinking I've got these great grades, but that's not the point. I'm not talking about now; I'm a whole lifetime behind."

But I wasn't thinking that at all. Instead, I was remembering that this was the very thing that had haunted me as a student, too, the sense that everyone around me—classmates, teachers, new friends—had a lifetime of reading books I didn't even know about, of going places and doing things that weren't on my radar screen. They grew up in families where books and ideas were a fundamental part of daily life. Except for schoolbooks, and later those I borrowed from the public library, I never saw a book in my house. Why would there be when my mother couldn't read?

I didn't know then that I wasn't alone in this experience, that it's the cost of mobility, the price one pays for moving across the border that divides the working class from the upper-middle-class professional life I entered. No one has recorded it better than Richard Rodriguez, who, in his moving memoir, *Hunger of Memory*, says of himself, "Always successful, I was always unconfident . . . the scholarship boy . . . [who] remains an uncertain scholar, bright enough to have moved from his past, yet unable to feel easy, a part of a community of academics."

I heard Delfina talking through the fog of my own thoughts. What could I say to her? I couldn't even reassure her that she'd one day catch up since I still feel I never have. It isn't just reading all the books you never read, learning to think the thoughts you didn't have. It's a whole way of relating to the world of thought, of being primed for it from birth on.

It's true that I have a whole set of experiences that most of my friends and colleagues, then as well as now, don't have and can probably never fully understand. And it's also true that those experiences give a unique cast to my work (from the subjects I choose to write about to what I have to say about them) that has helped my books gain wide acceptance. That's gratifying, of course. But there are still times when I see the depth of knowledge that undergirds the intellectual work of some of my closest friends, knowledge born of a lifetime of immersion in the world of ideas, that I feel again the sting of knowing I'll never catch up.

Delfina was scrutinizing me silently when I forced my mind back into the room. "What is it?" I asked. "You look as if you have a question."

She hesitated, then, "I was watching your face and wondered what you were thinking about because you looked so . . . you know, maybe upset or something."

I was caught. I didn't think we had yet developed the kind of relationship where self-disclosure was appropriate. But Delfina clearly knew something had happened to evoke strong feelings for me. To deny that, or avoid talking about it, would be to do to her what she had done first to Marianne and then to me. How could I complain about her behavior if I wasn't willing to act differently myself?

I took a deep breath and, hoping I wasn't too far off, told her the truth. "I was thinking about how much your experience mirrors mine and remembering that I had the same feelings then that you have now." I said that I, too, came from an immigrant working-class family; that, like her, I had a hard time believing in myself when I embarked on an academic career; and that while it has become a great deal easier, I still sometimes feel as if I'm faking it and fooling people.

I watched the play of expression across her face as I spoke, the furrowed brow as she listened uncomprehendingly at first, the dawning understanding followed by the look of amazement. She was quiet for several minutes after I finished speaking, taking in what I said, processing it. Finally, she spoke. "I can't believe it. You look so sure of yourself, like you always know what to say and do. I always thought people like you were born that way, you know, I don't really mean *born* that way but that it was just part of being American."

Being American—words loaded with meaning about identity, about the definition of self and place, about belonging. For me, in those early years when I was shamed by my family's foreign culture and language, being American meant not being Jewish. For Delfina, the meaning was complicated by race as well as ethnicity. For in a nation where skin color is a defining feature of one's person, being American means also being white, a border she could never cross.

"I know you're telling me the truth," she continued, "but I can't really believe you were ever like me. I feel so clumsy, like I'll never get it right, I mean, like I'm trying to get into a world where I don't belong and I'll never fit. These American students, they're so far ahead of me, I'll never be able to do it, never."

I knew there wasn't much point in offering what would feel like empty assurances to her; knew, too, that if she went on to graduate school, she'd be in a continuing struggle, testing herself and, even when she was doing well, fearing that she'd be found wanting, that she'd be exposed as the fraud she felt herself to be. It's why so many students of color drop out. Even when they have the intellectual ability to do the work, they lack the self-confidence to push through the hard times. When things get tough, they turn on themselves, convinced that the problem is theirs, that, as Delfina feared, they can never make up the deficits of their past.

I remembered how hard I worked as an undergraduate, fearful that if I let down for a minute I'd trip and fall. My daughter, a child of the upper middle class who was prepared for academic success from earliest childhood, was breezing through high school at the time. "Hey, Mom," she used to say, "let it go already. You know you've got your A, you always do." But *I* didn't know. *She* knew; she had a lifetime of knowing, of confidence born of being surrounded by books and ideas from the moment of birth, of knowing as far back as she could remember that she would go to college. As she puts it, "I grew up knowing that I'd always have enough to eat, a place to sleep, and that I'd go to college. It was as basic as that."

Delfina interrupted my thoughts, her words shy, diffident, a wholly different tone from the one I'd heard until then. "I have so many questions I want to ask you, but I don't know. Is it right? I mean, is it okay to ask?" She paused briefly, then with a rueful smile, "See what I mean? I don't even know what's the right thing here. I mean, the other one never talked to me."

I laughed. "There aren't any rights and wrongs here. No, I take that back; there's one *wrong*. You have to call me by name; I don't want to be *the other one* or *the new one* or whatever name you might devise. Apart from that you can say or ask anything. If I have a problem with it, I'll tell you; if not, I'll answer you honestly. And I'll expect that you'll do the same with me."

"What do I call you?" she asked, as if she didn't know my name.

"What do you want to call me?" I replied, knowing it wouldn't be an easy question for her to answer.

Years of interviewing people for one research project or another taught me how differently those of different classes and cultures respond when introduced to a stranger. When I walk into a working-class home, a professor from the university, I'm an authority figure, someone to be addressed respectfully by my full title, *Dr. Rubin*, even when I let them know I might prefer it otherwise. But in a middle-class household, I'm immediately welcomed as *Lillian*, a peer. It's the same with patients. Middle-class people often use my first name, even before we've met, as in a telephone message that says "Hi, Lillian, I'm Joe Smith; Mary Jones referred me, and I'm wondering if you have time to see me." But even after months or years in therapy, my working-class patients often have trouble using my given name.

I've seen it over the years in the African American community as well, neighbors, church friends, addressing each other as *Mrs.* and *Mr.* It's part of the culture, a statement of dignity and respect in a community of people who historically have gotten so little of it from the outside.

So I wasn't surprised when Delfina squirmed uncomfortably as she thought about how to answer my question, then said in a small voice, "I don't know."

"Since I call you Delfina, it seems right to me that you should call me Lillian," I suggested.

"I don't know if I can do that; I mean, you're older, not that I mean you're *old*, but . . . you know, you're a doctor and all that, and . . ." Her words trailed off in confusion and, much to her relief, we left it for another day because the session was at an end.

I was surprised when I saw her a week later. She looked larger, not just taller but actually bigger and more comfortable in her body. I don't just mean that she stood straighter, although she may have done that as well. It was more as if her internal sense of herself had shifted, allowing the withdrawn, hidden self I'd observed before to be replaced by a more open and available one. A change that was reflected in the way she carried herself. "You look different," I remarked as she settled in a chair.

"I do?" she said, taken aback. "I didn't know it showed, but I've been kind of excited this week, like thinking if you could do it, maybe I could, too." Then, as if she dared too much, "I don't mean I could be like you, it's just . . ." She stopped, unable to find the words.

"Just what?" I prompted.

"I don't know, I mean I never knew anyone who came up like you. I mean when you see it, it makes it seem possible."

"Yet, even though you had a child, you pushed on. Other sixteen-year-olds drop out of high school, but here you are finishing college and admitted to graduate school. It must say something about your aspirations. You didn't get here by accident."

She began to talk then, about how she always wanted to go to college and how hard it had been to actually make the decision to go when she'd been accepted. "You know, nobody ever went to college in my family," she said, as if that was an explanation.

"Can you say more about that?"

She looked at me for a moment, trying to decide how to respond, then retreated to a silence I thought she'd left behind. She seemed to shrink physically as she sank down into her chair and stared into her lap.

"Come on, Delfina," I coaxed. "Tell me what pushed you back into your corner?"

She struggled with herself, then still looking down at her

hands, said softly, "It's hard to talk about it. They didn't mean to be mean, but it was hard for them, like I was going away, or something, and they had to pull me back.

"I knew my mother was proud of me, but she was also mad, or maybe not mad, scared, like something was going to happen she didn't like. It was as if there were two of her, the mom who was proud that I was going to college and the one that didn't like the whole idea. I'd hear her on the phone talking to my aunts and bragging about Fina (that's what they call me) going to college. But when she got off the phone, she'd be on me about how I always had my nose in a book and didn't pay enough attention to my daughter. It was ridiculous because Mony (her real name is Ramona, but we call her Mony) was fast asleep by then anyway. Then she'd find something she needed me to do, and I'd have to leave off studying and do whatever it was right then."

Her words sent me back to my past once again, to my own mother's ambivalence about her Americanizing children. As I became increasingly comfortable in school and the world outside our home, my mother found more and more ways to clip my wings. "Educated dope!" she'd say scornfully when I said or did something she thought foolish or unwise. It wasn't just a cruel slap at a child. It was her way of protecting herself against her increasing sense of inadequacy before her American children, her way of managing her fears that we would stray too far. Fears, it turned out, that were well-founded, at least with her daughter.

It didn't get any better in adulthood. When I handed my mother my first published book, she said of this concrete symbol of the distance between our two worlds, "A lot of good it does me when you live three thousand miles away." She spoke of geographic distance, but we both knew she meant much more that. Yet she never gave up bragging rights in the public world. There, until the day she died, I was "my-daughter-the-doctor," spoken as if it were all one flowing word.

I turned back to Delfina, who was saying, "My mother would kill me if she knew I was talking to you about *la familia*. It's like that's sacred ground; you don't talk about the family outside the house, no matter what."

I told her I knew how hard it was to violate such family commandments, about how important family loyalty was in her community. "It's generally true in immigrant families," I said. "When people don't feel understood by the society that surrounds them, they cling to each other and don't want anyone to look inside. And I imagine it's even more so in the Latino community where so many people are undocumented and immigration agents are a constant threat."

A flicker of fear crossed her face. "We don't talk about that."

But over the course of the next weeks, she did, slowly and tentatively at first, talk about *that* and a lot more.

Her father worked in construction as a laborer; her mother was a housewife. For most of her life, the family lived in fear of the INS (Immigration and Naturalization Service), since her father had crossed the border illegally when he was thirteen years old. Except for some secret trips back and forth, one of them to marry her mother (also undocumented) when he was nineteen, he had lived and worked in California ever since. It wasn't until a few years ago when there was an amnesty, that he got a green card, then became a citizen.

No wonder Marianne saw Delfina as paranoid. After a lifetime of secrecy and fear, of knowing that an untoward word could bring catastrophe down on their heads, who wouldn't be wary of talking about the family to a stranger?

Neither of Delfina's parents had any formal education. Over the years her father learned English passably well, taught himself to read and write, and was literate enough to read a

Spanish-language newspaper but an English one was still a stretch. Her mother was wholly illiterate, and although she could speak a halting, heavily accented English when necessary, it remained for her the language of *los gringos.*

"If she ever heard us speak a word of English when we were kids, she'd have a fit," Delfina said. "'*Hablas ingles con tus amigos gringos, pero en mi casa hablas español!*'" she'd say. (Speak English with your *gringo* friends, but in my house you speak Spanish.) "It's why so many Latino kids have trouble with English; their parents make them feel like their committing a crime."

Knowing it might come in handy during one of our sessions, I had put Richard Rodriguez's *Hunger of Memory* in my briefcase after our last meeting. "I want to read something to you," I said as I pulled the book out and searched for the passage in which he writes compellingly about what he calls "the fierce power Spanish had" for his family and their friends. Even when they knew the language, they refused to speak English to him because for them "Spanish alone permitted our close association." In learning English he had "committed a sin of betrayal" against his family and "had shattered the intimate bond that had once held the family so close."

Tears streaked Delfina's cheeks as she listened intently, her head bobbing in agreement. "It's so true," she said excitedly almost before the last word was out of my mouth. "It's just what I feel, but I never heard anyone say it so beautifully like that. Do you ever get rid of it?" she asked, knowing there was no answer.

For Delfina, English represented a world beyond what she knew, a world she wanted to grasp, and precisely the world that the family injunction against English in the home was designed to keep at bay. "I'd try so hard sometimes to be like them, but I wanted something else, not that I knew what, except that I wanted to talk English like the American kids. But all it did was make me further from family. My sister and brothers, they didn't care, and anyway they just thought I was weird. My parents are good people, and my mother tried, but she didn't understand. To this day she doesn't really know me. It's hard for her, too; she complains a lot that I'm far away even when I'm there. And it's true."

It was impossible not to wonder, as I listened, whether her pregnancy at sixteen was some unconscious way of trying to fit in. Is she ready to hear this? I asked myself. She was a woman rooted in the present and its tasks, not inclined at the time to plumb her unconscious as deeply as I would have liked. But I felt certain she was sturdy enough to deal with whatever anxiety my remarks might generate and also that our relationship was strong enough to weather a mistake in timing. So I said what I was thinking.

She looked so startled I could almost see the thoughts churning in her head. "Do you think . . . ? I don't know; I was scared out of my mind; I thought my parents would kill me. Why would I do that to myself?" Then, without fully realizing the significance of her words, she answered her own question. "You know, the only time my sister and I were close was when I was pregnant. It's like I was like her then."

But that was as far as she could go.

As we continued to meet and our connection deepened, her anxiety abated, and she began to talk about going off the medication. I was afraid it was one of those miracle cures, what psychoanalysts call a "flight into health," and I was somewhat apprehensive about agreeing. But she kept telling me that she wanted to "test herself," that she had "to know whether I'm okay or it's just the meds."

I knew it was happenstance, of course, but in those moments, it felt as if some unseen hand had carried Delfina to my door. We might as well have been twinned, so closely did our lives parallel each other. I'd had the same discussion years earlier with my own therapist, not about medication but about my need to leave therapy for a while. It's characteristic of adults, who, as children always stood alone, to need the reassurance that they can still do it, even when they may not have to.

It seemed at times that I wasn't standing outside looking in, but was inside looking out, thinking what Delfina thought, feeling what she felt, seeing the world as she did. And as I had those many years ago. She was my past; I was her future. Only she didn't fully know it yet.

Enmeshed is the word I can hear some of my colleagues say as they read those words. A dirty word in psychological circles that describes people who are stuck together in pathological ways, people whose boundaries are so permeable that they have trouble knowing where one ends and the other begins. But I learned long ago that to get inside another's life as deeply as good therapy demands, I had to find the places where our two selves could meet. Lauren Slater, in her eloquent book about doing psychotherapy with schizophrenics, *Welcome to My Country*, makes the point compellingly when she writes, "There's no way . . . to do the work of therapy without finding your self in the patient and the patient's self in you."

I'm not saying that enmeshment isn't also pathological, only that what looked like enmeshment between Delfina and me could as easily be called *attunement*, that empathic, tuned-in response that's part of any good parent-infant relationship and that's a necessary accompaniment to the child's development. It's what helps the small child to see herself in the eyes of another, to internalize a world of warmth and understanding, a world where it's possible later to imagine others like herself. This is what Delfina didn't have at home; this is what she got from me, and this is what she needed to navigate the next big step in her life.

True, the line between *enmeshment* and *attunement* can be dangerously fine as we see in families all the time, and it requires care to keep from slipping from one to the other. But much of therapy is risky, this no more than many other situations we encounter. And here as always it's the therapist's task to monitor the transference and countertransference closely enough to minimize the risks, which, in this case, means making certain that the boundary between the two states remain firm enough to prevent slippage.

I supported Delfina's request for ending her medication with some trepidation, and for some weeks she did very well, continuing in her careful way to probe her internal life, to gain understanding, to sort out what of the issues she faced came from inside, what from outside—from pressure of family and community, from a society in which race and ethnicity counted so heavily in how she was defined, in how she defined herself.

Then she came up against decision-making time. Along with her acceptance to graduate school, she had been offered a fellowship, which would come close to supporting her first four years, and the promise of a teaching assistantship to cover the rest. She had waited until the last minute to respond with an acceptance, and they were pressuring her for an answer. If she didn't accept, there were others hungry to take her place.

She became more and more agitated as the deadline approached, and I feared she'd fall into a full-fledged panic attack again. "How can I do it? No one in my family even knows what a Ph.D. is. My parents have no idea what I'm talking about when I try to explain to them what it means. I mean, if I said I was going to be a doctor, they might think I'm crazy, but they'd at least know what I'm talking about."

"I know," I said. "It's a world so foreign to them that there's no way they can comprehend it. It's what upsets both of you, the knowledge that the gap keeps widening with every step you take."

We swapped stories for a while. I told her about how angry my brother became when I asked him to put off a proposed extended visit for a week or two because I had final exams and papers to write. "What the hell's that all about?" he shouted at me. "I can't come see my sister because she has homework to do."

She told me that her sister called her "a snob who thought she was better than everyone else" and hadn't talked to her for months.

I told her that when I called to tell my mother I'd graduated with a doctorate, she sniffed dismissively, "What kind of doctor are you? You can't even write a prescription."

She told me that her mother threatened to stop caring for her daughter unless she grew up, got herself a job, got married, and became a proper mother. "I know she won't do it," Delfina said, "she's too attached to Mony to do anything to hurt her. But still . . ." she concluded at a loss for words.

The more we talked like this, the more her anger surfaced and her resolve stiffened. Finally, she said, "Dammit, I don't care what they say; it's my life, not theirs. If I listen to them, I'll wind up where they are. I don't think I could stand it."

The next day she accepted her graduate placement with all its perks. She phoned me after she'd taken the plunge. "I just need to talk to someone who's glad for me."

It's years since that day, years during which I've remained some combination of booster, adviser, friend, mother, the person she turned to when the weight of her aloneness became too much to bear.

Over time, her fondest dreams and worst fears both came

true. She became a tenured professor at a midwestern university, a career that has given her much satisfaction but in which she still sometimes feels like a traveler in an alien world. "It's more subtle than feeling that I don't fit," she explains. "I think about how it was when I was a child in the barrio; at least I was comfortable in my skin then. I never felt like that again after I went to college."

Mony, her daughter, now a young woman, is an attorney doing public advocacy work in California. "She never had the same problems I did about moving between the two worlds. It's a different time, easier for these kids now. And it's a lot easier having a mother who understood what she wanted to do and encouraged her to go for it. I miss her now that she's so far away, but I'm so proud of who she's become. She's really a great person."

Delfina has had lovers along the way, but she has never married. "I was too busy earlier," she says, "and now I wonder. I don't exactly have regrets, but sometimes I wonder."

She talks wistfully still about missing the community of her childhood, her "innocence," she calls it, and tries to stay in close touch with her family. But they're not comfortable entering the world she lives in now, nor is she comfortable in theirs. "My life is so different, I might as well live on another planet. I still know theirs, but they have no idea about mine," she says sadly. "I mean the love is there, but except for family gossip, we don't have anything to share. Can I tell them about the article I'm trying to write that has me tied up in knots?

"You told me a long time ago that it's the price I would pay. I at least got something out of it, but I really feel for my parents. What did they get? A daughter they can't ever really know."

What Makes Therapy Work?

For most of my life I watched my brother, Len, crumble under the burden of poverty and pathology that defined our family life. As we grew into adulthood, there were times when he was able to stand upright, to live what looked like a normal life — work, marriage, children. It was as if he'd get pumped up for a while, then something would go wrong, and he'd deflate, sometimes slowly, like the air leaking out of a balloon left too long; sometimes like an explosion, fast and hard, the balloon popped by a pin.

He was in therapy on and off for more than twenty-five years, the last an unbroken fifteen-year stretch with a psychiatrist who saw him through three hospitalizations for agitated depressions so deep that he was unable to manage even the simplest tasks of living. Nothing worked for long, not talk therapy, not drugs, not electric shock treatments. After a third round of shock treatments did little to relieve his despair, he found his own way out — an automobile accident that was quite clearly a suicide.

I spoke with my brother's therapist, sometimes in person, more often by telephone, whenever a crisis arose. He was a kind man, calm (too calm, I thought), reflective, and well schooled theoretically. But he had that air of professional detachment so many therapists cultivate as a way of maintaining the boundaries between self and other, a manner that was all professional sympathy and enigmatic "hmmmms" and nods that left me wondering who he was and what he heard.

My brother, the child of a father who died when he was six years old and a mother whose most accessible emotion was pathological rage, lived encased in emotional isolation. It was

154

obvious to me that he yearned for something different. Why else would he have spent so many years in therapy? But he couldn't, didn't dare, come close enough to anyone to risk another loss, another humiliation, another physical or verbal beating. All his life he was enmeshed in relationships that, whether with our mother or his wife and children, he could never fully enter and never finally leave. Not surprisingly, he replayed the same scenario of enmeshed isolation with his therapist, never wholly comfortable with either staying or going. Unfortunately for him, he wasn't enacting the script alone.

There were periods in his therapy when he was ready for something more and willing to take the risk to get it. But there was no one on the other side of the interaction to meet him there. "I don't know why I go," he complained during one of those times. "He never says anything, and when he does, it's never anything I want to hear."

"What do you want to hear?"

"I don't know; I want him to be human. Who knows, maybe I want him to love me," he answered, in an unusual burst of openness and insight.

"There's nothing wrong with that; tell him how you feel," I urged.

But each time he tried, he was met with an interpretation about looking for his lost father, or his anger at his mother, or his own problems with intimacy. The interpretations weren't inapt; these were, indeed, issues Len needed to examine and come to terms with. But a smart interpretation that ignored the need my brother expressed, an interpretation that turned his very human and adult wish into a childlike problem, was the last thing he needed at the time.

Would his life have ended differently if he'd been in therapy with someone who believed as much in the power of the relationship as in analyzing a patient's pathology, a therapist who could respond openly to his patient's criticism, examine his own behavior, and consider whether his unrelieved professional disengagement was, in fact, the best stance for this particular person? I don't know. But I do believe that for Len to have had a chance, he needed what Irvin Yalom has called so pithily, *"the therapeutic act, not the therapeutic word."* Only with someone who had the capacity to enter into an authentic relationship, one who saw therapy as two equal participants in a struggle to solve the problems before them, could my brother have had the kind of corrective emotional experience necessary to make his way through the pain and sorrow that dominated his life.

For what makes therapy work is, indeed, the therapeutic act. Any therapist can give words to her understanding, can find "reasons" for the neurotic problems she sees, whether someone else's or her own, reasons that may even be correct. It's a central part of the job description, what all psychotherapists of any discipline are trained to do. But it's not reason that accounts for that indefinable something, that near-mystical affinity that bound and held any of the people I've written about in this book in a therapeutic relationship through some very hard and frightening times. It was the relationship, what I did, who I was in the room, not what I said, interesting and enlightening though my words may have been. And no less important, it was their ability to accept and use what I offered.

Interpretations have their place and sometimes even provide an "aha" experience, that moment when the patient hears something that's so true it feels as if light flooded a darkened room. Unfortunately, it takes time to *know what we know,* to integrate the knowledge so that we can actually use it. The moment of "getting it," therefore, is often soon followed by a long period of "forgetting it." Who among us, we who have been patients as well as therapists, doesn't know that experience? Who hasn't found herself asking, "Where did it go? I had it; it was right, I know it was, but it's gone."

I recall my first visit to my own therapist, a wise older woman who seemed to look into my soul. At the end of the hour during which I recounted the key elements of my past and present, including the retelling of some of my "bad mother" stories, she looked at me quietly and said, "I think you've spent your whole life running as fast as you can to ward off depression. It must be exhausting."

If anyone had told me before that I was depressed, I would have thought them daft and pointed to my busy and productive professional and personal life. Love and work — according to Freud the two central arenas of life that need resolution. And I had it all. But in that moment of blinding clarity, I knew she was right. My mind stood still as I comprehended the words and felt the relief that swept over my body. Someone cared enough to see and name this thing that had driven me all my life. I collapsed into gut-wrenching sobs that came from some-place inside me I didn't even know existed.

But while the moment remains vivid in memory decades later, the "aha" didn't translate into an immediate ability to change my life. It was only a beginning, the beginning of *knowing but not knowing*, of taking two steps forward and one step back. And even now, all these years later, my epiphany about my tendency to depression hasn't stopped it from set-tling in on me from time to time, a dark veil that drops over my eyes without warning, clouding my vision, so that the same life that seemed bright and inviting yesterday looks dreary and unwelcoming today.

The difference between then and now is that I no longer need to ward it off in ways that were themselves problematic. I can let it happen with the knowledge that it's a mood, not real-ity, that it won't drown me or force me into some depths from which I can never return. It's still not easy to live through the bleakness. But now I know as surely as I know I'm writing these words that I'll wake up one day and, in the same mysterious way the veil came down, it will lift, and the world will be bright again.

Until then, I still take refuge in my work at those times, but not with the frenzied, dervish-like quality I lived with before. Now, too, I'm able to allow friends and family to be there with me through the dark periods in ways I couldn't before a therapist helped me learn about trust, not by any words she spoke, but by who she was and what she did, a woman who, although a classically trained psychoanalyst, had the wisdom to set aside the rules and offer the kind of relationship she knew I needed. She was the "good mother" I never had, the mother who was always on my side, who wanted to know who I was, who cared about what I thought, who was interested in my work, who read my books, and who in a hundred subtle and not-so-subtle ways let me know she cared.

When I look back over that time, it's not her theoretical sophistication I remember, not her keen observations, but the warmth of her wise, caring eyes, her encouraging smile, her unmistakable concern for me, not just as a patient but as a woman she respected, and not least, her honest confrontations when she thought I needed a jolt. Was some of what I experienced then transference? Certainly. But there was also reality, for she was a strong and articulate presence in the room, a therapist who, whatever transference/countertransference issues surely existed, allowed an authentic relationship to flower between us. And in the final analysis, it was that relationship that healed.

I said in the opening pages of this book that in the reciprocal dance between mental health professionals and those who become our patients, they expect more than they should, and we promise more than we can deliver. Too often, therefore, people come into therapy looking for that magical moment, that instant when everything falls into place and they are transformed, their struggles vanquished. It's an illusion buried deep in our psychological culture, aided and abetted by media accounts of drastic transformations and by a society that insists we can master any problem, climb any mountain, if only we have the will and the wit.

Yet, in reality, even in those relatively rare instances when the magic happens, it's only a beginning; the real work lies ahead. For if, as I believe, the task of therapy is to lay the groundwork and teach the skills for a continuing struggle for self-awareness — the necessary prelude to the kind of growth and change that enables us to manage ourselves and our world more effectively — there can be no moment of ultimate understanding that relieves all pain, no final "click" that says "I'm done."

Indeed, no matter how hard we work, no matter how much we learn about ourselves, no matter how we rewrite the narrative of our lives in the course of therapy, we leave it as we entered, changed somewhat, yes, but also the same — the same history and the same unique constellation of character, personality traits, and experience that, together, make us who we are. Even when therapy works most effectively, the most we can expect is to come away having learned how to live more easily with ourselves and, therefore, with others. Then the same situations that might have disabled us before will no longer carry the emotional power to disrupt our lives, whether internal or external. But, for good or ill, the soul and spirit we bring into therapy leave with us.

Freud himself knew there was no cure and no transformation, only the possibility of transcending. Which is why he promised only to turn neurotic suffering into ordinary pain. How does one cure life and the problems it throws up at us when we least expect them? How do we cure our existential angst over such things as loving, living, and dying? How, indeed, can anyone cure us of whatever combination of life experience and inborn qualities went into making up who we are? The best therapy can do is to help us know ourselves better, to accept what we know, and give us the tools to change or moderate those parts of ourselves that hinder our ability to live, work, and love productively — in itself no small accomplishment.

Acknowledgments

First and foremost, my gratitude goes to my patients who allowed me the privilege of sharing their lives, then permitted me to write about them. Without them, this book could not have been written. Therefore, it is to them that I owe my deepest debt, one that I can repay only by honoring not just the content of their stories but the spirit of their lives and struggles. More than anything else, I have tried to do just that.

There are always people who stand behind the author of a book—family, friends, and colleagues who provide emotional support while also reading, discussing, and criticizing the work in progress. For their generosity of both intellect and heart in these behind-the-scenes roles, my thanks to Bob Cantor, Joan Cole, Diane Ehrensaft, Peter Finkelstein, Dorothy Jones, Michael Kimmel, Nancy Lucas, and Gail Mason.

Kim Chernin, who has been close to this work since it was little more than a poorly articulated thought, has left a significant mark on the finished book.

Barbara Artson, with whom the line between friend and family was long ago blurred, deserves special mention, not just for what she contributed to the book but for what she adds to my life.

Rhoda Weyr, as much friend as literary agent for the last thirty years, deserves rave reviews for her performance in both roles.

It has been a pleasure to work with my editor, Helene Atwan, who is blessed with the grace that makes even tough criticism easy to hear.

Thanks, too, to all the others at Beacon Press who nurtured

Acknowledgments

this book from its earliest production stages to its birth with unfailing courtesy and efficiency.

Last but not least there is my family—Marci, Larry, Blake, Margaret, Edward, our newest and most welcome addition, and most of all, my husband, Hank, an unfailing partner in all arenas of my life for forty wonderful years. Without their love and support, life itself would be less possible.